Experiencing hardship is hard and can often overwhelm us. Yet it is a means God uses to shape us. *Resilience Rising* helps us to see how that can be and gives many practical tips for developing a mindset that allows hardship to do its persevering work. Practical and to the point, this is a helpful guide to surviving what often is a persistent part of life.

Dr. Darrell L. Bock, Executive Director for Cultural Engagement of the Hendricks Center and Senior Research Professor of New Testament Studies at Dallas Theological Seminary

Feeling overloaded, nerves fried, resilience failing? In his book *Resilience Rising,* seminary professor Scott Barfoot serves as a trusted guide helping readers to find their strength in God, developing endurance through life's most fiery trials.

Dr. Sandra Glahn, seminary professor and multi-published author

In today's chaotic world, leaders face added challenges both personally and professionally. Adversity and suffering either take us down or ultimately build us up—but we all need help to reframe our afflictions into strengths, endurance, and resilience. God has provided that assistance through Scott Barfoot's stellar new book. He defines resilience as, "the art and science of a mindset shift that transforms the heat and stress and friction life brings into a source of hope and renewal..." It's rich with biblical examples, deep spiritual insight, and stories and illustrations to encourage the discouraged. What a gift to a friend or family member going through a season of struggle—and with time, I suppose that's just about all of us!

Dr. Sue G. Edwards, Professor Emeritus, Educational Ministries and Leadership, Dallas Theological Seminary, and co-author of *The Discover Together Bible Study* series

Resilience Rising by Scott Barfoot is a practical and insightful work on how to find strength and resilience amid insurmountable circumstances. Scott's approach is insightful and full of personal stories. It's like talking with a good friend about life's challenges on a cold, winter night—and the fireplace and conversation warm your body and spirit. As Scott relates: "What could be worse than being blind?" Helen Keller replied, "To have sight without vision." Resilience Rising has vision to embrace.

Very nice work—readable, approachable, practical, biblical and warm.

Dr. David Fletcher, Founder, XPastor

As leaders, we all go through challenging experiences that often break us. With great insights, Dr. Scott Barfoot discusses Biblical principles to encourage us to press on with resilience through our most difficult times and thrive. These principles are practically illustrated through wonderful stories, impactful anecdotes, and personal experiences. I highly encourage every leader to read this book!

Dr. Stephen G. Tan, Senior Pastor, Grace Christian Church, Philippines

Long-term thinking is useful for strategic leadership. Resilience, more than mere thinking, calls us to long-term living in faith and faithfulness. With insight gleaned from biblical characters, personal experience, and ministry leaders, Scott Barfoot provides pastoral steps and practical stops for spiritual leadership. And if you don't need biblical wisdom immediately, read this book anyway. You might soon need such encouragement, as I did and still do in the face of unexpected and unsolicited adversity.

Dr. Ramesh Richard, President, RREACH; Professor, Dallas Seminary; Founder, TOPIC, Convener, GProCommission

Resilience Rising is a powerful guide for anyone facing life's most challenging seasons. With practical biblical wisdom and real-life examples, this book equips readers to not just survive any adversity but to rise above it, finding strength, perseverance, and refreshed faith. This book is a must-read for anyone seeking lasting resilience in the face of hardship. What I especially love about Scott's work is his consistent use of the Scriptures to take the reader back to bedrock principles.

Dr. Rod MacIlvaine, Founding Pastor, Grace Community Church, Bartlesville, OK Scott Barfoot has written an immensely helpful book for all of us! Right now, I am praying daily for four friends dealing with cancer and have seen church planters and pastors deal with unbelievably difficult personal, family and church situations. Life is often hard, and Barfoot brings us rich encouragement through the scriptures and his personal stories and practical exercises. From babies looking like shriveled raisins to messy woodworking, Barfoot's words will bring you encouragement and a pathway to resilience!

Dr. Bob Rowley, Former District Superintendent, EFCA Texas-Oklahoma; Adjunct Professor, Dallas Theological Seminary

RESILIENCE RISING

*Finding Your Way Through
Life's Toughest Moments*

D. SCOTT BARFOOT

Klisia

Plano, TX

2024

RESILIENCE RISING

*Finding Your
Way Through
Life's Toughest
Moments*

D. SCOTT BARFOOT

Resilience Rising: Finding Your Way Through Life's Toughest Moments

Klisia
Plano, TX
Klisia.org

Editor: Murilo R. Melo
Copyeditor: SooJin 'Anica' Tan

Publisher's Cataloging-in-Publication Data
provided by Five Rainbows Cataloging Services

Names: Barfoot, D. Scott, author.
Title: Resilience rising : finding your way through life's toughest moments / D. Scott Barfoot.
Description: Plano, TX : Klisia, 2024.

Identifiers: LCCN 2024946843 (print) | ISBN 978-1-961349-08-7 (paperback) |
    ISBN 978-1-961349-06-3 (ebook) | ISBN 978-1-961349-07-0 (audiobook)

Subjects: LCSH: Discipline--Religious aspects--Christianity. | Perseverance. | Spiritual life. |
    Church work. | Biblical teaching. | BISAC: RELIGION / Christian Living / Spiritual Growth. |
    RELIGION / Christian Ministry / Pastoral Resources. |
    RELIGION / Christian Living / Personal Growth.

Classification: LCC BJ1533.C8 B37 2024 (print) | LCC BJ1533.C8 (ebook) | DDC 248.8/42--dc23.

"to my wife and best friend, Debbie, and our three incredible kiddos, Davey, Joel, and Karissa, all whom love, teach, and challenge me on my journey through hardship toward Christlike resilience…"

"to those remarkable servant leaders from across the globe who despite adversity, faithfully and sacrificially serve Jesus in their small corner in God's grand vineyard…"

CONTENTS

BEGINNINGS

"Many men [and women] owe the grandeur of their lives to their tremendous difficulties."

— *Charles H. Spurgeon*

❧

Leaders all around us are buckling under the pressure of tremendous hardship. But does it have to be this way?

What if the challenges you face today are the very steppingstones that will lead you to a faith stronger than you ever imagined? Do you long to navigate life's obstacles with resilience, embracing them as opportunities for personal growth and transformation?

No one who holds the mantel of leadership denies that it carries enough burdens by itself. Like Frodo as he takes the heavy One Ring to rule them all, you know the unrelenting mental, emotional, physical, and spiritual stressors caregivers for the soul bear, often alone.

Like so many of us, you are on a quest to find your way through the looming darkness, lurking dangers, and exhausting terrain of unimaginable hardship—those closest to your heart depend on it. You are courageously committed to the people you love and the cause you champion. That is why you want to know the secret to resilience in the face of life's most daunting turn of events so that nothing precludes you from completing God's mission.

Life is Tough

Resilience is the ability to effectively adapt to and bounce back from disorienting adversity.[1]

Over the past sixteen years, I am humbled to have worked with hundreds of leaders from dozens of countries serving on the frontlines of ministry. While many of these dear servants live and breathe resilience in adversity, many flounder, longing to find their way through hardship.

My heart yearns for these incredible men and women as I consider their stories, and I can worry about their well-being as I do for my own family. The experience of personal hardship and suffering makes a person more sensitive to the needs of others and more empathetic because, in so many ways, you are right there with them in their journey of faith through hardship.

I spoke at a men's discipleship gathering at our church some time ago. We were studying the book of James. As I introduced my talk on James 1:1–3, "My brothers and sisters, consider it nothing but joy when you fall into all sorts of trials, because you know that the testing of your faith produces endurance." I said, "Hi, my name is Scott Barfoot, and my middle name could include the initial 'H' for hardship—Scott Hardship Barfoot—because my life has been full of hardship and trials. Perhaps just like yours."

As I went through a litany of my many hardships over the years, I saw the men nodding their heads in compassion and agreement. I told them about the time of our eldest son's labor and delivery when at birth, during an emergency cesarean-section, he experienced oxygen deprivation and couldn't open his eyelids until his first surgery at three months old.

I briefly mentioned the terrorist attacks of 9/11 while I was living just miles from the Pentagon. And shortly after, the frightening Washington, D.C. sniper assaults of 2002, where six persons were randomly killed in our neighborhood. I told them about the time I was so physically

---

1 American Psychological Association, "Building Your Resilience," n.d., https://www.apa.org/topics/resilience/building-your-resilience.

and emotionally exhausted that I burned out and how our pastor was a source of encouragement.

I talked about when my wife, Debbie, was in a severe car accident and the other driver, who was unlicensed, was suing her for several million dollars. Also, the traumatic experience of walking with our dear friends in the sudden loss of their eight-month-old son. Then the season when my two younger sisters, one after the other, were diagnosed with two different, aggressive forms of cancer, with one passing away at the early age of 44, leaving behind her husband and ten children.

And presently, the ongoing challenge of caring for aging parents with significant physical and cognitive decline. The list goes on.

My heart resonates with those on this same journey as they find their way through hardship.

I think of the Louisiana pastor who returned home following a powerful hurricane only to find a towering 50-foot pine tree had split his house in half. And to make matters worse, the insurance company denied his coverage.

Or the missionary family in Asia who sacrificed a decade to learn the local culture and language only to be told by the regional government officials to pack their bags and immediately leave the country.

The Latin American denominational leader who lost his beloved brother—a local church pastor entrapped by a complicated ring of gang violence.

I remember learning about a student ministering in northern India and his arrest for sharing the gospel while experiencing debilitating health challenges.

Or when I sent a quick email to leaders in China asking how they were doing, and their curt reply was, "It's complicated."

The stories of hardship are familiar and often raw. Even as we emerge from the global pandemic, many faith leaders, missionaries, church planters, pastors, chaplains, and healthcare workers have been running at warp speed in crisis mode for far too long. Their adrenaline is running in short supply, some are experiencing health setbacks as a result, and many are discouraged—struggling with fatigue, depression, and hopelessness.

You carry your burdens and know firsthand how life's raps knock the wind out of your sails, leaving you overwhelmed, under-supported, and powerless. Perhaps, this may be one of the reasons you are reading this book with a mix of curiosity and desperation.

So when life gets tough—and it does—how do some leaders find remarkable strength and resilience through seemingly insurmountable circumstances?

Join me on my journey through hardship as we explore this question and discover from Scripture how the Lord uses unimaginable adversity to strengthen personal resilience—a resilience that helps us rise above our circumstances, overcome the ensuing darkness, and stay the course to accomplish God's mission.

Mindset Shift

As we begin our journey through hardship, we must start with a mindset shift in understanding, approaching, and responding to life's perpetual stressors. An automotive engineering breakthrough gives us a clue.

One feature that has taken the automobile industry by storm over the last decade is the genius of regenerative braking systems. The automotive braking mechanism had two primary goals: 1) slow down the vehicle by applying friction between the brake pad and the wheel disc, and 2) dissipate this friction-produced energy to prevent the wheel from overheating.

The regenerative braking system by design made an intriguing shift from questions concerning kinetic energy diffusion to kinetic energy transformation. In other words, engineers went beyond asking how to diffuse this energy from the brake-produced heat and friction to how to harness this power for greater purposes, such as recharging the EV's battery.

This automotive industry paradigm shift mirrors what needs to happen as we find hope and renewal when confronted with adverse, demanding, and traumatic situations.

I'm allergic to pain, just like you, and my first choice is to avoid it at all costs. I can think of a pain-generating problem in the church or at the seminary, and my gut instinct is to say, "Lord, let's just make this all go away!"

But as you know, most problems won't just evaporate into thin air due to my wishful thinking or urgent prayer—they must be addressed. So I may try to minimize the problem.

"Maybe this issue isn't that big of a deal," I think to myself. "A couple of conversations, an apology or two, bringing a peace offering to the offended, or some other form of appeasement can solve the problem."

Here I move from total stress avoidance to distress minimization. Of course, for some ministry situations, I might be tempted to go the other extreme and engage in the classic bull-in-the-china-shop approach to overcoming adversity.

Here I confront the issue head-on (which can be a good thing) but lack Daniel-like skill in approaching the person or situation with wisdom and tact. Whether this approach is the making of a dominant personality type, pride, or reactive impatience, this knee-jerk reaction fails to address the real issues. It could then inadvertently reduce the problem to something less than it is, creating a whole new set of problems.

The real challenge, notwithstanding, is that the old mindset needs to shift to something new. Our highest priority is not to live a comfortable life with the ultimate goal of dissipating all experiences of leadership heat and friction. Our primary goal is not to avoid, minimize, or oversimplify adversity to its lowest common denominator.

Leaders need to learn (and relearn) the art of transforming the kinetic energy of hardship in a way that reenergizes them and their service with renewed strength, wisdom, and resilience as an engine for pursuing the mission of God.

The incessant strain of life's daily grind all while being broadsided by an unexpected crisis doesn't have to wear me down or burn me out. These stressors can be the instrument that recharges my battery, keeping me humble, teachable, curious, compassionate, and flexible, inspiring me toward the new horizons God has for me.

Today's most tenacious servant leaders are discovering the art of resilience through ancient biblical wisdom applied to their harsh realities of frontline leadership and ministry.

These rich scriptural precepts can help leaders navigate their past, present, and future challenges with grace and hope, and demonstrate how to harness adversity for healthy change, growth, and transformation.

A Pathway Forward

So, how do leaders find strength and personal resilience through seemingly insurmountable hardship?

First, strengthening personal resilience requires a mental shift to accept hardship as an ally rather than an enemy. Every crucible experience is a gift from the Lord to refine, revitalize, and renew our faith in our good and great God.

Second, through the lens of God's Word, we will journey through hardship, highlighting key life-giving practices that can expand our resilience capacity by reflecting on the life and leadership of some of our greatest heroes of the faith.

No matter how difficult, daunting, or despairing life gets, it doesn't have to take you down. It is in this place of unthinkable hardship where the Lord breaks us to make us better, humbles us to build us up, and burdens us to make us stronger, forming in and through us something more than we could ever imagine.

CHAPTER 1

ALWAYS REJOICE

(Romans 5:3–5)

Not only this, but we also rejoice in sufferings, knowing that suffering produces endurance, and endurance, character, and character, hope. And hope does not disappoint, because the love of God has been poured out in our hearts through the Holy Spirit who was given to us..— Romans 5:3–5

REJOICE IN YOUR SUFFERING AS GOD USES IT TO PRODUCE
PERSEVERANCE, CHARACTER, AND HOPE.

If anyone found his way through unrelenting hardship, it was the apostle Paul. As the Lord promised, trouble followed Paul wherever he went throughout his dramatic life.

In his passionate plea to the Corinthians, the apostle takes his readers through his resume of tireless labor for the gospel's sake. For Paul, dire circumstances didn't hold him back one inch from his mission of proclaiming Christ to the nations.

It didn't matter whether he was unjustly imprisoned, beaten, flogged, whipped, or stoned. It didn't make a difference if he was snake-bitten on occasion or shipwrecked three times. The constant danger from thuggish bandits, his own countrymen, the Gentiles, or the false brothers didn't deter him from doing what was right.

Those times of not knowing where he might get his next meal or his next thirst-quenching drink of clean water, or when he shivered for days, ice cold for lack of clothing and shelter, did not break his spirit. Time after time, Paul encountered near-death experiences that only cemented his resolve.

Over and above all this, Paul described one of his heaviest burdens of concern. He longed for the flourishing of all those followers of Christ who were like his own children, who struggled with pressing spiritual burdens among the churches to which he wrote (2 Corinthians 11:22–28).

Paul's unstoppable, unflappable, dogged determination to accomplish God's gospel mission is breathtaking. No matter the cost. No matter the sacrifice. No matter the persecution. No matter the trials. No matter the setbacks. Paul remains firm.

If Paul were here right now, I could see him lean over your shoulder and whisper, "Come on, my friend. Yes, what you are going through is extremely difficult. I certainly understand. But it is a normal part of our broken, upside-down world. It is a sign that God loves you and is helping you become all that he wants you to be. Trust him. You are not as big as you think you are. Humble yourself and learn the lessons he has for you."

On our journey toward resilience, we can't help but to ask these questions: *What was Paul's secret? Was there something about his mindset that kept him focused on the goal rather than succumbing to despair? What was the underlining element of his inner fortitude that ensured a spiritual and mental elasticity to help him not merely endure such relentless trials but to rise above them with remarkable resilience?*

Paul in his own words reveals the answer: "*We also rejoice in sufferings*" *(Romans 5:3).*

Rejoice in our sufferings. Really, Paul?

The apostle echoes this same sentiment to the Philippians while imprisoned: "Rejoice in the Lord always. Again I say, rejoice! Let everyone see your gentleness. The Lord is near!" (Phil 4:4–5). So also does James, the half-brother of Jesus, when he encourages the isolated Jewish believers to "consider it nothing but joy when you fall into all sorts of trials, because you know that the testing of your faith produces endurance" (James 1:2–3).

On the one side, God's shining, good, gracious, and empowering presence radiates through Paul's darkest tribulations, and on the other stands the fruit of his kindness through a series of most excellent and praiseworthy outcomes. In other words, as bad as it seems, it isn't that bad compared to the surpassing goodness and greatness of our God at work behind the scenes and the amazing work in you and through you he is going to accomplish.

In Romans chapters 4 and 5, Paul highlights the astounding good that can emerge from our suffering and hardship. For Paul, hardship is the refiner's fire that melts adversity in all its pain and anguish and recycles it into a growing faith that is renewed and more resilient.

In the crucible, Paul holds on to the nearness and goodness of God, who can take all the pain and hurt, all the physical, emotional, and spiritual brokenness. Every single stressor. And mold it into something great, beautiful, and life-empowering. Paul doesn't cower in fear, grumble in bitterness, or despair in hopelessness. He rejoices and calls his readers to rejoice with him. He beckons us to always rejoice, to keep our chins up, our smiles wide, our kindness consistent as we journey through hardship.

The story is told of a young boy who courageously but unsuccessfully attempts to move a heavy log to clear a path to his favorite fort.

His dad stands quietly next to his son, watching him strain against the weight.

After a few moments, he says, "Son, why aren't you using all your strength?"

Befuddled, and quite flustered, the boy remarks, "Dad, I'm using every ounce of strength I have!"

There is a silent pause.

"No, son. You are not," his dad gently responds. "You haven't asked me to help."[2]

We strive. We struggle. We push. We press. We try everything on our own strength. And then we hit the wall. We have a choice. We can keep trying to move the log of our suffering by our own strength—exasperated, worn out, depleted, discouraged. Or we can stop. We can ask the Father to help.

I love what Bill Lawrence often taught his students over his many years of teaching at Dallas Seminary: "God has called you to do that which you cannot do with the resources you do not have for the rest of your life."

Isn't that the truth!

Paul is right. We *can* rejoice in our sufferings! We don't wallow in them, hide from them, work around them, or fend them off in our own strength. We have a loving heavenly Father who is right there with us in the midst of the crisis, and it is this same God who was right there with Paul and Abraham throughout ages past.

Rooted faith in our good and powerful God helps us walk through the valley. It helps us stand firm in the fire. We can surrender and find peace in the loving arms of our master even as he holds us in the flames, as he heats and hammers us into something greater.

Suffering Produces Perseverance

Paul further accentuates the reasons why we can rejoice in our suffering: *"because we know that suffering produces perseverance."*

One of the benefits of life's tests and trials is the development of a tough, enduring, and steadfast faith. Not only a faith that rests in the power of God, but also a faith that bounces back from setbacks and failure. In other words, a faith that is so glued to God's loving character and promises as recorded in the Scripture that no heartbreak can pry it from

---

2 Ken Boa, "40. Healthy Alliances | Bible.Org," https://bible.org/seriespage/healthy-alliances.

us. No disillusionment can cloud our ultimate allegiance. No fear can restrain us from a full-throttled, wide-open, growing and vibrant faith.

This is the kind of resilience Paul calls us to.

Perseverance means we lean into the grace and power of the resurrected Lord Jesus Christ. It is the ability to rest in him as we bear up under intense pressure in his strength with patient resolve and undeterred persistence to push against the descending burden, obediently doing the right thing.

I remember some time ago watching a highly accomplished bodybuilder friend demonstrate a feat of incredible strength as he bench-pressed 300 pounds at the YMCA. I thought either his arms were going to collapse or the bar was going to break!

On his third and final repetition you could see his muscles tense and his veins pop. The blood rushed to his face. He grunted, slowly pushing up with all his might under the intense resistance to complete his final set.

I was amazed at how he could bear up under such excessive weight. He assured me it didn't happen overnight but was a part of a disciplined regimen over many years of diet (he eats eight eggs for breakfast every day!), exercise, sleep, and hydration.

Suffering, like weightlifting, contributes to a personal resilience which can not only carry us through our journey of hardship but over time expand our capacity to endure the resistance and stress that a broken and fallen world can bring.

Perseverance Produces Character

Paul asserts not only the reward of perseverance through suffering, but also that this perseverance produces a secondary celebratory benefit. The apostle notes that "*suffering produces perseverance, and perseverance, character.*"

This certainly was the case for Paul.

First, Paul's call to gospel ministry was inaugurated with suffering.

The Lord expressed to Paul through Ananias that his new life of faith in the resurrected Jesus would be full of suffering (Acts 9:16). This suffering resulted in Paul's salvation and his sanctification. For the sake of the gospel, it made him into the godly and instrumental man that God wanted him to be.

We can't forget that before his conversion, Paul was known as Saul. He was a part of the Jewish religious elite, a high-ranking Pharisee from Tarsus who prided himself in the persecution of Christians in the early church. Right there at the stoning of Stephen, Paul provided his full approval of this merciless execution (Acts 8:1).

And yet God in his grace and power rocked Paul's world, struck him like lightning on the Damascus Road, knocked him off his horse, and stunned him blind (Acts 9). Like a form of boot camp, the Lord threw him on his back for three days of utter hell and helplessness. He couldn't see, eat, or drink anything (Acts 9:9). We know from medical science that the human body cannot withstand much more than three days without hydration. The Lord brought this hardened man to the point of death—and it wouldn't be the only time—to gain his attention and arrest his allegiance.

It is significant that the Lord used intense physical suffering to bring this proud and evil religious leader to his knees. The Lord first had to break Paul to build him up into the godly man and servant leader he wanted him to be, no longer persecuting the church (Acts 8:3; 9:1–2) but preaching the gospel to all the nations (Acts 9:19–20).

In other words, no suffering, no apostle Paul. Think about that for a moment.

The same holds true for you. No suffering, no you. Yes, it is hard. Yes, it is filled with hurt, and pain, and disappointment. But you are what you are because of it. While suffering in the past has left its scars, has not the Lord used it to make you better—to make you stronger, wiser, more compassionate, and even more effective in the place he has called you to?

For Paul, this dramatic suffering was just the beginning of God's work to create in him a resilient resurrection faith for a lifetime of gospel service.

Paul's whole life was filled with one unthinkable hardship after another. It was through this process that the Lord galvanized his perseverance, honed his character, and forged in him an unbending resilience and unwavering faith of total dependence in God alone.

The apostle pens these penetrating words in his letter to the Corinthians:

> For we do not want you to be unaware, brothers and sisters, regarding the affliction that happened to us in the province of Asia, that we were burdened excessively, beyond our strength, so that we despaired even of living. Indeed we felt as if the sentence of death had been passed against us, so that we would not trust in ourselves but in God who raises the dead. (2 Corinthians 1:8–9)

Note the emphasis on "affliction that happened to us," "burdened excessively," "beyond our strength," "despaired even of living." But then also note the development and strength of his character in verse 12, "For our reason for confidence is this: the testimony of our conscience, that with pure motives and sincerity which are from God—not by human wisdom but by the grace of God—we conducted ourselves in the world, and all the more toward you." (2 Corinthians 1:12).

Paul suffered a ton, and this suffering propelled him toward "pure motives" and "sincerity" in the wisdom and grace of God. But it wasn't a stroll in the park. It was a battle between his flesh and the Spirit (Rom 7). Paul describes this tension as he reflects on his experience of receiving special "visions and revelations from the Lord" that bent him toward sinful pride and boasting.

In his grace, the Lord gave Paul a perpetual form of suffering that wouldn't go away. He called it "a thorn in the flesh was given to me, a messenger of Satan to trouble me—so that I would not become arrogant.. I asked the Lord three times about this, that it would depart from me" (2 Corinthians 12:7–8).

This thorn was nothing less than unimaginable, ongoing, mind-numbing pain. We don't know what it consisted of, whether a physical ailment or a besetting temptation, but Paul found supernatural strength through this inner suffering just as he did through the many external hardships.

Paul continues,

> But he [the Lord] said to me, "My grace is enough for you, for my power is made perfect in weakness." So then, I will boast most gladly about my weaknesses, so that the power of Christ may reside in me. Therefore I am content with weaknesses, with insults, with troubles, with persecutions and difficulties for the sake of Christ, for whenever I am weak, then I am strong. (2 Corinthians 12:9–10)

Christ's power rests on Paul, so Paul's power can be found in weakness as he rests on Christ. Paul suffered repeatedly. And yet he perseveres in the grace and strength of the Lord.

Paul knew firsthand how, for the gospel's sake, the Lord used his sufferings of all kinds to bring him to faith, produce perseverance, and refine his character to make him more and more like Christ.

Paul contends for the priceless value of journeying through suffering and hardship as it yields a treasure trove of courageous perseverance and God-glorifying character maturation, leading to a more unshakeable resilience.

Character Produces Hope

The apostle continues to call us to rejoice in our sufferings since they result in such life-giving and transformative outcomes. Picture a series of dominos standing on edge, one next to another. When pain is inflicted, it first produces perseverance; then perseverance, character; and character, hope.

Hope is the next benefit of our sufferings. Hope is like oxygen. We can't go very far without it. Hope nurtures resilience through hardship.

And resilience through hardship nurtures hope. Hope does not let us down but assures us that God, in his goodness, is working out his divine purposes.

I love Paul's description of Abraham's hope-filled faith in the Lord when both Abraham and Sarah felt as good as dead in their old age and their inability to conceive a son. Paul writes, "Against all hope, Abraham in hope believed and so became the father of many nations, just as it had been said to him" (Romans 4:18, NIV).

Winston Churchill's leadership during the horrendous atrocities of the Second World War was one that modeled extraordinary hope—a hope that was against all odds. Many during the war believed Britain was doomed by the onslaught of the German Nazis. Churchill, however, characteristic of his bulldog spirit, against all hope, persuasively exudes hope in his June 4, 1940, House of Commons speech, *We Shall Fight on the Beaches.*

> We shall go on to the end, we shall fight in France, we shall fight on the seas and oceans, we shall fight with growing confidence and growing strength in the air, we shall defend our Island, whatever the cost may be, we shall fight on the beaches, we shall fight on the landing grounds, we shall fight in the fields and in the streets, we shall fight in the hills; we shall never surrender, and even if, which I do not for a moment believe, this Island or a large part of it were subjugated and starving, then our Empire beyond the seas, armed and guarded by the British Fleet, would carry on the struggle, until, in God's good time, the New World, with all its power and might, steps forth to the rescue and the liberation of the old.[3]

The author of Hebrews articulates a hopeful faith so succinctly. "Now faith is being sure of what we hope for, being convinced of what we do not see. For by it the people of old received God's commendation." (Hebrews 11:1-2).

---

3 Winston Churchhill, n.d., https://nationalchurchillmuseum.org/we-shall-fight-on-the-beaches.html.

Paul was no different than Churchill or Abraham in how his hardships and sufferings cultivated perseverance, character, and hope because he knew "that all things work together for good for those who love God, who are called according to his purpose" (Romans 8:28).

🖤

Mindset Shift in Trials

- Make a list of those things that bring you joy, purpose, meaning, and hope despite adversity.

- Block out an afternoon to reflect on Paul's and Abraham's journeys of faith, and observe how they matured through trials, setbacks, and failure. Consider your own difficulties and how you can reframe obstacles as a catalyst for spiritual strengthening and growth.

CHAPTER 2

LOVE WELL

(2 Corinthians 1:3–4)

*Blessed is the God and Father of our Lord Jesus Christ, the Father of mercies
and God of all comfort, who comforts us in all our troubles so that we
may be able to comfort those experiencing any trouble with the comfort
with which we ourselves are comforted by God.* — *2 Corinthians 1:3–4*

LOVE OTHERS BY BEING A CONDUIT OF THE LORD'S
COMFORT THROUGH YOUR OWN HARDSHIP.

❦

I will never forget the births of our three children. While each of their stories is unique, they share a common thread. In a hospital nursery, newborns line the room in rectangular cribs. In my humble opinion, every single one of these babies, with no exception, regardless of the hospital or where they were born, look like shriveled raisins.

But not my three! They were beautiful.

I remember holding them after their delivery, next to Debbie, overlooking their screeches and squeals with chins a-quivering and hardly noticing their kicking little arms and legs in seeming protest until securely swaddled. At that moment, time stood still. They were stunning, treasured, and loved.

And as their daddy, I had the privilege of welcoming them into the world—a strange new world with masked doctors a-prodding. A world of mystery, pain, and change. What an opportunity to pour out my love. To care for and comfort each of them in their moment of great need and vulnerability.

Like a loving father with his newborn, God's love tempers our suffering and distress with his kind, gracious, and merciful ways. God's love stands with us as we bear the pressures of life's burdens. God's love helps us receive the trials and tests that prove his character and refine ours. God's love fills our hearts and minds with hope against all hope that helps us rise above the tragedies and tears—just like the apostle Paul. God's love helps us suffer well, to love well.

That's what makes Paul's thoughtful words in his letter to the Corinthians so poignant.

> Blessed is the God and Father of our Lord Jesus Christ, the Father of mercies and God of all comfort, who comforts us in all our troubles so that we may be able to comfort those experiencing any trouble with the comfort with which we ourselves are comforted by God. (2 Corinthians 1:3–4)

Suffer Well. Love Well.

Resilient leaders recognize the value of personal hardship as the very thing that qualifies them to love well.

The love of Christ compelled Paul to live not solely for himself and his own needs and desires but sacrificially for the Lord Jesus Christ and his gospel purposes for the Corinthians. Even as some were questioning his credibility and attacking his character, the apostle, in humble strength, articulated his sincere and persevering love for them. Paul loved regardless of his most trying circumstances. Paul's suffering gave him credibility as he called his readers to follow his example of gospel-love.

Not like the world's love characterized by selfishness and self-preservation, but like Christ's love. Selfless, self-giving, and sacrificial. A love set apart, holy, generous and rich, full of mercy, kindness, long-suffering, and patience. A love that pursues and restores and hopes.

Without those difficulties found in adversity and suffering that a sinful and broken world brings, we cannot fully comprehend how much God loves us, shriveled face and all.

And if we don't fully experience God's love, it will be impossible to truly love ourselves as cherished children made in the image of God, our loving heavenly Father. If we are not secure in our sense of identity as God's beloved children, we will fall far too short in our ability to be a conduit of love to those he brings across our path.

Paul suffered well. But he also loved well.

A Beautiful Mess

The love of God is overwhelming for Paul in the gospel. There was something beautiful to be found in the messiness of suffering—a treasure to be cherished, a truth to hold on to, a future reality that kept him grounded with unrivaled hope. It was more than just his secret to personal grit and strength of character.

Several years ago, I was visiting with a colleague at the seminary. His office was a modest-sized room with a rectangular executive desk on one side next to his office chair. Then there was the *wow* moment. It wasn't a window with a view nor a novel piece of technology sitting on the desk, and it certainly wasn't the drab carpet. It was a side table—a stunning work of art.

As you enter his office, to the left against the wall, parades a beautiful, wooden, hairpin-legged table. It has a natural live edge with smooth and rounded contours and showcases his beloved family and his exceptional carpentry skills. The captivating natural wood grains stand out under the meticulous finish.

I commented on the table's beauty and received a quick lesson in woodworking. It inspired me to build my own live edge console table and, most recently, a dining table bench.

As an amateur like myself, building live edge furniture is a creative and beautifully messy process. This is especially the case when the wood is so worn and distressed that epoxy is required. I've used epoxy on a couple of projects in the last year. There are certain types of resin that, when hardened, aesthetically blend in with the wood.

This messy process includes several steps:

First, assuming the piece of wood has been cut to size, you rough sand the surface areas on both sides of the slab. Next, seal the bottom with painter's tape so that epoxy won't inadvertently leak through to the floor. Finally, mix the resin, the dye, and the hardener, pouring it into the cracks, crevices, and damaged areas of the wood.

The epoxy in its liquid form can easily spill over onto the tabletop surface while filling the wood's fissures and gaps. It can be cleaned with a damp cloth. No need to be concerned about the excess as it can be removed later. Once this step is complete, let the resin dry for a good 24-48 hours. At this stage, the tabletop looks dreadful, with random globs of semi-transparent hardened epoxy splattered on top. In fact, at first glance, someone off the street might see that the wood appears to be botched and either trash it or chop it for burning.

Next, you remove the excess epoxy with mask and goggles on. Depending on the size of the project and how many areas need the epoxy, scraping and sanding can take a significant amount of time, requiring strength, skill, and patience. The sanding process will leave you sweating, muscles fatigued, and with a mask coated in sawdust. But once the surface and edges are sanded smooth, the wood surface is wiped down, and the Danish oil applied, that slab of wood metamorphoses into a beautiful work of art.

Paul recognized that there is something beautiful in every season of hardship, every affliction, and every setback in suffering. It is more than mere survival, and it is more than withstanding intense amounts of pressure and pushback. There is an opportunity to discover God's tender-hearted love as he is the "Father of mercies" and "the God of all comfort." And it is in this loving comfort that we are empowered to love well, one of the essential elements for a resilient faith and another reason to always rejoice in our sufferings.

Every hardship is God's opportunity to show us his mercies, demonstrate his compassion, rest our fears, and soothe our heartache in such a way that we are not only blessed but can bless others in the same way—that we can love well.

It was this same kind of thinking that led engineers to shift from kinetic energy diffusion to kinetic energy transformation. This same mental reframing made Paul stronger, wiser, and more full of faith in a good God through the winding road of adversity.

The burden of our afflictions can be more of a blessing than we might realize. In the heat of the difficult situation, we can experience the grace and power of God's comfort in a transformative way for helping others find solace, patient endurance, and hope through the dark night of the soul. And in doing so, we become more resilient, which helps us help others persevere through their plight.

I will never forget my high school gym class the year we learned how to wrestle Olympic-style. I was a short, skinny teen at the time, and other than my feet of about a size 12, I had not yet gone through my full adolescent growth spurt.

During the class, we learned and practiced various holds like the Far-arm, Near-ankle, Half-nelson, Cradle-pin hold, and more. There was one other formidable technique that helped me push through to victory.

It was the day we experienced actual teacher-refereed wrestling matches. I paired with Chris, who was a couple of years older, as strong as an ox, and double my size and strength. We sparred across the mat as our teacher and classmates watched. I was flailed around by my opponent like a stuffed rag doll. And then, I remember, he put me into a half-nelson. I was on all fours—the thick blue floor mat below us. Chris positioned himself next to my left side. Like a pry bar, he wove his arm under my left armpit and over the back of my neck. As he pried, trying to flip me on my back, he moved his right hand, attempting to lift my left leg simultaneously. I resisted with all the might I could muster. I knew I couldn't hold him long. And then the *eureka* moment came—the *reversal technique*. So I continued to resist his aggressive half-nelson hold as he put all his strength and the support of his legs behind it. Then suddenly, to his surprise, I completely relaxed my resistance. In my weakness, his energy alone provided enough momentum to roll me over on my back and then to keep rolling me back up, right on top of my opponent for the winning pin.

That day, the thing I feared—my opponent's strength—became the exact thing I needed to win. All that affliction and trouble of being thrown around like a stuffed animal was paramount for my success, and it just had to be harnessed and redirected. I had to learn how to be a conduit of all that power.

When stress comes at us fast and hard, it can strengthen our resolve not just to survive or even thrive but to find the love of God, the master of all comfort, and extend that loving compassion and consolation we experience to those that come after us. And there we can find victory and experience the reversal effect.

Master of All Comfort

Paul praises God as he opens his letter to the Corinthians, declaring him the master of all comfort, "who comforts us in all our troubles." No matter the trouble or the hold the enemy seems to have us in. No matter how great, how ordinary, or how insignificant the trial. No matter the cause of the affliction or the duration of the danger. God's consolation encourages us in our distress.

Paul's winsome words to the Corinthian Christians are crucial for us today, "For just as the sufferings of Christ overflow toward us, so also our comfort through Christ overflows to you." (2 Corinthians 1:5).

God calls us to do more than solely dissipate adversity's heat and friction. He calls us to recycle our afflictions for his glory, our good, and the benefit of others. The apostle Paul calls us to follow the example of Christ. To join him in the fellowship of his sufferings, to become a master comforter and a mindful encourager who serves as a conduit of compassion, understanding, empathy, encouragement, and support for those fellow sufferers he brings across our path.

So, how was Paul comforted by the Lord? 2 Corinthians 7:4–7 gives us some insight into this vital question.

Paul writes,

> I am filled with encouragement; I am overflowing with joy in the midst of all our suffering. For even when we came into Macedonia, our body had no rest at all, but we were troubled in every way—struggles from the outside, fears from within. But God, who encourages the downhearted, encouraged us by the arrival of Titus. We were encouraged not only by his arrival, but also by the encouragement you gave him, as he reported to us your longing, your mourning, your deep concern for me, so that I rejoiced more than ever.

Incredible. Paul was "filled with encouragement" and "overflowing with joy." How? The faithful, struggling Corinthian believers at some point brought comfort to battle-scarred Titus. Perhaps they provided a place of refuge for Titus to recharge after a long and exhausting season of ministry. Maybe they prayed with him, asked him how he was doing, about his family and his mentor, good old Paul. Perhaps they fed him and tended to his physical needs. Clearly, through their comfort, Titus recharged his spiritual batteries and God used him to encourage Paul, delivering the message of the Corinthians' loving concern for him.

Paul, was so depleted after being "harassed at every turn" with "conflicts on the outside" and "fears within," that God knew he needed encouragement. How amazing to see the love and comfort of Christ come full circle.

Something healing takes place as we share from the overflow of our sufferings in those divine appointments. And then, when God leads us to a person going through something quite similar, it reminds us that there is purpose and meaning so clearly evident that only the Lord could orchestrate it.

Perhaps, like me, you have found yourself asking God why all the perplexing hardship.

My wife, Debbie, and I sure did when our eldest son was born with a complex syndrome involving an anomaly of the eyelids. Then, even after several surgeries, some unsuccessful, to learn that there is a possibility that his condition could, down the road, lead to significant visual impairment or even blindness (which, while proofreading this text, Davey indignantly points out, proved to be false!).

Before Davey's first surgery, a couple in our church brought us comfort. The husband, a medical doctor, was taking turns with his wife holding Davey at our church home-group gathering. They intently observed and studied him and expressed concern for us and Davey's visual health. And then, one of them commented that we were a special couple that God would entrust Davey to our care.

These were agonizing days, months, and years for us. But the Lord was teaching us how to release our illusion of control, receive his love, and be his conduit of compassion. God longed for us to grow in our ability to console others in their journey through heart-gripping hardship.

And at the same time, things don't always have a silver lining or make sense. We wrestle with the mystery of God's allowing and doings. There are also times when the Lord seems unusually distant or even absent in the middle of our distress as we call out for his rescue. But even in disappointment, we learn we are not alone and can cultivate a spirit of trust, rest, and peace because we know God is with us in the uncertainty and ambiguity.

Suffering teaches, prepares, and qualifies us to love others well. It gives us the key to enter their world, validate their pain, and join with them in God's gospel story. It equips us to be conduits of comfort and encouragement, just like we have received.

Shared suffering reminds us we are not alone. We can assure others that they are not alone in their time of lament as we stand with them in courage, with a heart of compassion, seasoned with empathetic listening and gentle questions that draw them out, and a pastoral presence that creates a safe restorative place. It is a place filled with beautiful messes.

By God's grace, even with additional burdens that Davey has had to bear over these last twenty-one years, God is developing him into a fine young man. In recent days, Davey's unique experiences has equipped him to love and serve his grandparents unconditionally.

The other evening, Davey volunteered to help Grandpa and Grandma connect their laptop to their television to stream a worship service. A task that normally takes a few minutes somehow stretches into more. Before long, a couple more requested "minute" tasks becomes an hour or two. Loving unconditionally and with patience in the face of the cogitative decline that has come with age is no small task, but Davey seems to have the capacity more than most.

Each visit and conversation leaves you unsure of how they might respond or think or say. Sometimes they are aware and sharp, then a few minutes go by, and they are in a completely different reality. But for Davey, these relational dynamics don't detract from his heart of care and ability to demonstrate loving kindness to his grandparents.

As I was thinking and praying the other day, I couldn't help but praise God for his goodness and grace. Despite many challenges, Davey approaches life with a growth mindset. He is both highly visual and an astute observer of patterns. His sister notices that Davey "sees" things others don't. He holds himself (and his parents!) to a high standard. He is teaching himself Greek and studies the Bible with intense focus and attention to detail that would rival a seminary professor's. We continue to love and pour ourselves into Davey through prayer, discipleship, and church. And now he comforts us as he loves his grandparents in ways we cannot.

What is remarkable is that Debbie's parents helped us in those difficult years after Davey's birth. They were godly, faithful prayer warriors and huge ministry supporters. They poured into their first grandchild, Davey, and into us. And now we are giving back to them, and their grandson Davey and his two other siblings are sacrificially ministering to them in cadence with the example they had set. It takes a village not just to raise a child—it takes a village to help loved ones grow young.

Shared experiences of suffering and comfort in the context of a trusted community of fellow sojourners are so sacred. It is a gift from heaven with the power to comfort, deliver, and produce "patient endurance" (2 Corinthians 1:6) for those who participate. When we share in our sufferings with compassionate sympathy toward one another, it fosters an eternal perspective for the giver and receiver. It fills our souls with overflowing hope, inward renewal, and personal resilience.

❦

Mindset Shift in Trials

- Journal for 20 minutes about a time when you felt God's comfort in a profound way. Describe in detail those moments you sensed his abounding love.

- Brainstorm practical ways you could share these experiences to support and encourage a family member or close friend going through difficult times.

CHAPTER 3

STAY FOCUSED

(Hebrews 12:1-3)

Therefore, since we are surrounded by such a great cloud of witnesses, we must get rid of every weight and the sin that clings so closely, and run with endurance the race set out for us, keeping our eyes fixed on Jesus, the pioneer and perfecter of our faith. For the joy set out for him he endured the cross, disregarding its shame, and has taken his seat at the right hand of the throne of God. Think of him who endured such opposition against himself by sinners, so that you may not grow weary in your souls and give up.— Hebrews 12:1–3

FIX YOUR EYES ON JESUS AND HIS EXAMPLE OF

RUNNING THE RACE WITH PERSEVERANCE.

O n our journey through hardship, we've learned from the apostle Paul to always rejoice, knowing that God purposes our suffering to foster endurance, encourage godliness, and instill hope. Second, we've discovered that adversity teaches and qualifies us to be a conduit of his love, calling us to comfort others in their suffering just as we ourselves have been comforted. In this chapter, we turn our attention to Jesus and his heroic example of running the race with perseverance.

The Christian life is like an agonizing race. While it certainly has its share of 100-yard dash events, for most of us this race is marked less by short sprints and more like a long marathon—an extended race with many checkpoints along the way.

Successful runners, just like my weightlifter friend at the YMCA, require tremendous discipline including an intensive exercise regimen, a supporting diet plan, adequate sleep, and a mental grit that fortifies their determination to win.

During the race, contenders make every effort to remove anything and everything that might impede their performance. This includes what they wear and how they groom. However, while these externals can be important factors for success, the internal alignments are far more critical.

Every good coach knows this all too well. You can have a skilled and gifted runner, but if they lose their focus, lack the mental toughness to push through the pain, or hold anything less than a hopeful attitude regardless of how they might feel under the pressure, it could be the difference between winning, losing, or even dropping out of the race.

Run with Perseverance.

That is why the author of Hebrews, like a good coach, reminds us to eliminate anything and everything that might hold us back from running the race with every ounce and fiber of our energy, focus, and endurance.

And while throwing off all hindrances, we are also called to fix our focus like a laser. Not on our opponents, not on the length or intensity of the event, not on those entanglements we've thrown off, or the pain we might endure. Instead, these things should help us to zero in on Jesus, the author and perfecter of our faith. We are to look to him, consider his suffering, meditate on his example of perseverance as he ran the race set before him. Only then can we learn the art of resilience and find our way through hardship so that we do not grow weary and lose heart.

First, we are to "get rid of every weight and the sin that clings so closely" (Hebrews 12:1). Can you imagine showing up at the gym with your trainer, arriving bright and early at 5:00 a.m. sharp. There you stand decked out in denim blue jeans, steel-toe work boots, and a heavy leather motorcycle jacket. "Okay, Coach," you say. "I'm ready for today's run!"

Running an intensive race is not sustainable if we are bogged down by burdensome encumbrances. Please understand that there is nothing sinful about jeans or leather jackets or steel-toe boots. Some of the things holding us back from the race set before us may be good things. The good, however, can keep us from the most excellent.

The late Fred Smith Sr. uses the analogy of a garden hose. He suggests that many of us are like water sprinklers. We have too many holes, spraying everywhere but lacking power and impact. He argues that we must learn focus. When a garden hose has only one hole and a nozzle at its end there is a tremendous, controlled power that can be used with precision and resourcefulness.

In the Christian life there are the good things that may keep us from what is most excellent and praiseworthy. These need to be addressed so that we can run the race before us. It is equally true that we need to "throw off the sin that so easily entangles" us (NIV).

A hardened heart of disobedience is a detriment to the spiritual runner. Some of us may be like this. We show up to the race not only wearing jeans, boots, and leather jacket, but our ankles are half tied together with rope, leaving us hobbling onto the track. And then there are these cool sunglasses that blind our vision. And then on our arms are handcuffs. Oh, you know, you were experimenting with them and you lost the key and didn't have time to get the wire cutters to remove them.

I can't help but chuckle at this caricature of a straitjacketed runner in training. Extreme? Yes. Funny? Kind of. But sad, really. Why? Because this is the reality for so many. We must guard ourselves, or we too could fall into this pattern of trying to live the Christian life, trying to run the race with endurance only to find ourselves exhausted before the first mile marker and foolishly wondering why.

There is no way you and I can run the agonizing, intense race set before us when our soul is weighed down by all these encumbrances. Throw them off. Get rid of them. Recycle them. Donate them. Have a garage sale. Give them away. Release them. Turn away. Repent. Prepare yourself to run the race with grace, power, and laser focus.

Fix Your Eyes on Jesus.

Here is an important lesson: we address sin, but we don't wallow in it. We don't fix our eyes on the sin that so easily entangles. We don't fix our attention on the things that hinder our ability to run the race. We throw off all that stuff and move forward. But to what?

The author of Hebrews does want us to fix our eyes on the Lord Jesus Christ. He wants us to consider him and how he ran the race marked before him with perseverance. Roy Gingrich expounds,

> We must keep on looking to Jesus, *the beginner* (originator) and *the finisher* (completer) of our faith. *He is the One who originates our faith, the One who maintains our faith*, and *the One who brings our faith to completion* (our faith will be completed when we reach the goal, possess the inheritance). Only Jesus can keep our faith blazing as *the Devil, the world*, and *the flesh* try to extinguish it with the waters of error, worldly pleasure, and discouragement.[4]

How did Jesus run? Hebrews 12:2 gives us a hint. First, there was "joy set before him." Jesus knew who he was. He knew all authority had been given to him. He knew who would deny him and betray him. He knew his purpose to glorify his Father. He knew his mission as mediator to take on the sin of the whole world—your sin and mine—to satisfy the wrath of God (John 13:1).

Though perfect, innocent, and God-incarnate, Jesus longed for the redemption of humanity for those that would place their faith him. He longed for the joy set before him, knowing that the final victory of his sacrificial love would outweigh the heart-wrenching cross, its shame, and

---

4 Roy E. Gingrich, *The Book of Hebrews* (Memphis, TN: Riverside Printing, 2004), 55.

the painful betrayal he would experience from sinful, broken people. The struggle was real but the joy of knowing the final outcome was greater.

I can't help but think of my wife, Debbie. She bore our three children, suffering a grueling first half of her pregnancy with extreme and debilitating morning sickness for all three. When pregnant with our daughter, she literally lost 12 pounds in a matter of weeks, unable to keep food and liquids down. Her acute weight loss and physical depletion even startled her close friend who came to visit. But it was God's grace, a lot of prayer, and the joy that was set before her that strengthened her to labor in love, to push through the pain, and to give birth to three amazing persons.

Every mother, as every athlete knows the adage: "No pain, no gain." That's why folks bear children and join cross-fit or martial arts or other sports where they submit their bodies to some pain and duress for a greater purpose. They gain resilience in part because of the goals they aspire to.

"How was your workout?" you might ask a friend after his stint at the gym. "It was great," they reply. "I'm just a little sore."

Or "Congratulations on the birth of your first grandchild! How is everyone?" "Mom and baby are doing fine, though they are just a little exhausted."

Jesus ran with perseverance as he knew the end game and the joy that came with it. New birth, new life, new hope, and new possibilities for sinful and broken people. But the race set before him came with such a high cost as he endured the cross, scorning its shame. In other words, Jesus' race was an agonizing one filled with much pain.

As we fix our eyes on Jesus, we are compelled to consider the pain he endured for our sake. It helps us disentangle our spirits from the pain we often bear as a result of a fallen and broken world.

The Problem of Pain

In his darkest hour, Jesus experienced horrific abuse as he walked down the winding Via Delarosa ostracized, spit upon, brutally beaten, rejected by the masses, and betrayed by even his closest friends.

This pales in comparison to the agony of bearing the sin of the whole world—your sin and mine—on his shoulders to satisfy the wrath of a holy God. And yet this greatest agony would be his greatest act of love. It was his love that invigorated him with unbelievable joy. This inner delight for our good empowered him to endure to ultimate victory over sin and death, rising to sit at the right hand of the throne of God.

Hebrews v.3–4 underscores Jesus' overwhelming pain and suffering. "Consider him who endured such opposition from sinful men, so that you will not grow weary and lose heart. In your struggle against sin, you have not yet resisted to the point of shedding your blood" (Hebrews 12:3–4).

Our pain is real. There are times when our pain can be excruciating regardless of whether this was the result of sinful men or our own foolishness. Our pain may be frightening, disheartening, frustrating, and exhausting. But as we focus our vision on Jesus and how he ran his race we are encouraged to keep on and not stall out from fatigue or discouragement.

A popular story is often told of a compassionate lady who approached Helen Keller. Feeling sorry for her seemingly hopeless condition of blindness, she asked, "What possibly could be worse than being blind?" To which Helen replied, "Only one thing is worse and that is to have sight without vision."

As we fix our gaze on Jesus and his example of obedience amid terrible anguish, we must consider how to navigate our unique experiences of pain with the determination and perspective of Helen Keller.

It is likely that you have experienced or know of someone who has tasted heart-rending pain like Doctor Luke describes in his gospel concerning Jesus as he agonizes and prays in the garden to the point of sweating blood.

Pain has a way of hijacking our subconscious. It shapes our thinking, the values we hold dear, the mindsets we nurture. It can condition the countenance we carry, what we believe and how we behave, and the relationships we foster. Our experience of pain speaks to our emotional and physical wellbeing and the vibrancy of our spiritual life.

The problem with pain is not limited to the painful event itself. The challenge is in how it is understood, managed, and directed. Or said another way, how I perceive and respond to a particular traumatic event can either curdle my soul or cure it.

Jesus models for us something neuropsychologists call emotional regulation as we struggle with pain. This is where we learn "how to gain mastery over one's internal sensations and emotions" in the face of highly demanding and stressful situations. If our default physiological responses take over, traumatic experiences may push us into a fight, flight, or freeze response that can leave us "enraged, shut down, overexcited, or disorganized." [5] When Jesus is in the garden, we catch a glimpse of his final lap in the race on earth when he prays to the Father, "Not my will, but your will be done." In the garden Jesus explores his deep emotions and inner turmoil in the crucible before him and finds support and courage from the Father. He surrenders his present and anticipated burden.

> Social support is the most powerful protection against becoming overwhelmed by stress and trauma. Social support is not the same as merely being in the presence of others. The critical issue is reciprocity: being truly heard and seen by the people around us, feeling that we are held in someone else's mind and heart. For our physiology to calm down, heal, and grow we need a visceral feeling of safety. No doctor can write a prescription for friendship and love: These are complex and hard-earned capacities.[6]

We see in the example of Jesus, one who uniquely responds to the horrendous cross event before, during, and after in such a powerful way. Granted, he was sinless. He was God incarnate. Yet, he was fully human as we are and tempted in every way just like us. There is an empathy and

---

5 Bessel van der Kolk, *The Body Keeps the Score: Brain, Mind, and Body in the Healing of Trauma* (New York, New York: Penguin Books, 2015).

6 Bessel van der Kolk.

an encouragement from Jesus and his example to work our way through pain and suffering toward intimacy with God and obedience to his call.

Let us indeed fix our eyes on Jesus, the author and perfecter of our faith, and his example of running the race with perseverance.

Mindset Shift in Trials

- Spend a few minutes before you go to sleep reflecting on Hebrews 12:1-2. In solitude and silence, remove all distractions as you consider what weights and entanglements are hindering you in running the race.

- Meditate on the gospel accounts of Christ's passion this week as you go through your day. Focus your thoughts on Jesus' resilient love, trust, humility, and obedience.

C H A P T E R   4

DEEPLY TRUST

(Exodus 14:13–14)

*Moses said to the people, "Do not fear! Stand firm and see the
salvation of the LORD that he will provide for you today; for the
Egyptians that you see today you will never, ever see again. The LORD
will fight for you, and you can be still." — Exodus 14:13–14*

DEVELOP A GROWING CONFIDENCE IN THE
SOVEREIGN CARE OF A GOOD GOD.

❧

Years ago, my wife and I took our two boys for a swim at the community pool.

I had been teaching my oldest son, Davey, who was about four at the time, to tread water. I took him out to the five-foot deep area. This was well over his head but not over mine. He truly wanted to go deep to learn more about swimming and yet he was really frightened of the water.

At one point he started screaming as he clung to me like Gorilla Glue. He was desperately afraid that I would let go of him and that he would sink to the bottom of the pool and drown.

After a struggle to pry the little monkey off my neck, I was able to set him up on the concrete side of the pool wall. Only his feet were in the water as he sat there at my eye level.

I looked into his eyes and then said in a gentle but firm voice, "Davey, I love you and I promise I will not let you fall in the water. Do you understand? I promise, I will not let you go!"

There was a moment of quiet, and then something magical took place.

Davey slowly slid himself back into the deep waters and into my arms. He didn't scream. He didn't panic. He listened. He trusted.

Davey replaced his fear of the deep waters with an even deeper faith in the power and presence of his dad.

As I reflect on the drama of that day with Davey, I can't help but see a reflection of my own struggle. You know what I'm talking about. We somehow get into the deep end of the pool and know we are in way, way over our head.

And yet right there with us, God stands holding us in the water. He looks us in the eye and says, "I love you. I promise I will not let you go. I will never leave you nor forsake you."

Today there may be an area in your life where you feel totally overwhelmed because of the deep waters you face.

Rest assured nothing is over God's head. He is in control and is calling you to deeply trust him.

In his amazing grace, the Lord aspires to build in us a deep, vigorous, and resilient faith—an unshakeable confidence in his personal presence, awesome power, and abounding goodness.

A faith so rooted, we grow to receive hardship as a gift from God that strengthens our perseverance, refines our character, and rivets our hope. Our journey through trouble qualifies us to love well, calling us to fix our eyes on Jesus and his example of running the race through the pain with joy and endurance.

This faith is something we are to cherish, hold personally and tightly, and yet hold freely so that we can give it away, passing it on to our children and their children's children, to future generations.

It is a multilayered approach framed through the transcendent lens of eternity. The Lord's redemptive plan is the same yesterday, today, and tomorrow, even as it spans the ages and threads through the generations. He is a loving heavenly Father with great power embodied in whole-hearted love, pursuing his broken and needy children, longing for their redemption, yearning for them to reciprocate his devotion through an unbending allegiance to his majestic person and pleasing purposes.

In other words, God lovingly labors through both the mundane and those momentous moments to transform our faith, teaching us to trust him deeply.

God's laboring love is no different for us today than it was for Moses and the Hebrews during their 400 years under the rule and reign of Egypt. For the many generations after Joseph's journey from the pit of brotherly betrayal to years of gut-wrenching, humiliating hardship in a foreign land to his anointed rise to power as second in command of all Egypt only to rescue his family and people from inevitable famine and death. What man meant for evil, God transformed for good.

Forgetfulness, however, metastasizes and the subsequent Egyptian generations forgot Joseph's story. But not the Hebrews, who had now grown to be as numerous as the stars.

The Hebrews' faith in the Lord—the God of Abraham, Isaac, Jacob, and Joseph—was cocooned for generations in the mundane daily hardship of slave life in a very pagan culture. Then, at the Lord's appointed time, in his compassion, he preserved, prepared, and called Moses as his chosen servant to lead the people of Israel from the bondage of Egypt to the promised land. A move from the mundane years of day-in day-out slavery to the monumental, tumultuous moment. God took Moses and the Hebrews to the impossible places where he taught and tested and tempered resilient faith so that his people would learn to deeply trust him. This process of trust-deepening is multilayered. It is both personal and communal for Moses, the Israelite people, Paul, Abraham, and us.

It is in the impossible place that God works out his incredible purposes. There he teaches and tests, tempers and transforms our faith. He makes us into something more, forging a resilient, deeply trusting faith, steeled for his glory, our good, and the benefit of future generations. Imagine.

Have you ever wondered why God has brought you to this impossible place? It may be because the Lord wants to cultivate a renewed faith forged in the fire. Confidence purified from self and pride, fear and anxiety, discontent and greed, disappointment and disillusion. A faith more fortified, more vibrant, more sure, more centered, more dependent, more humble, more powerful, more beautiful, more hopeful, and more trusting than ever before.

He Teaches Faith

When the Lord led Moses and the Hebrews from Egypt, he took them the long way around the desert toward the Red Sea (Exodus 13:17-18). The Lord knew the Hebrews were not ready for war with the Philistines, which was likely if they were to follow the shorter route through Philistine territory.

Here the Lord led the people of Israel to a uniquely prescribed place— the place of the impossible. And it was not just any impossible place, it was a special place—personalized, customized, tailored— to teach his children to trust him more.

How encouraging!

It reminds me of the story of the dad who took his school-aged daughter grocery shopping. She volunteers to carry the grocery items her dad selects. As they approach the checkout line, the cashier says to the young girl under a towering load of groceries, "Sweetie, you are carrying an awful lot of groceries. You better be careful, you don't want to hurt yourself." To which the daughter replies, smiling at her father. "No, Ma'am, I won't hurt myself. My daddy knows how much I can carry."

God knows how much we can carry! As our loving heavenly Father, he will never thoughtlessly burden us. The Lord, by divine design, tailors the hardships we face, and he customizes them to cultivate a resilient, enduring faith that will bring us to new horizons.

As the Lord led Moses and the Hebrews to the impossible place of the Red Sea, the Lord strengthened their faith and Moses' leadership credibility. He not only wanted to tailor their hardship to teach them trust, but he used this space to test the substance and quality of their faith.

He Tests Faith

It is under the intense pressure, extreme tension, and red-hot fire of the crucible that tests faith's mettle.

In Exodus 14, Moses courageously follows the Lord's loving leadership right to the edge of the Red Sea. As they wait there, the Lord hardens Pharaoh's heart: "What have we done? We have let the Israelites go and have lost their services!" (Exodus 14:5).

Pharaoh, Egypt's proud ruler, mobilizes his lethal army, including 600 of their best chariots. They pursue Moses and the Hebrew people to the shores of the Red Sea.

The Lord guides them to this impossible, unthinkable place. They are between a rock and a hard place, on the edge of doom, and their demise is seemingly imminent. Suppose they try and swim through the Red Sea, and they drown. Or if they stay and try to fight, they die. What if they surrender—at worst, death, at best more years of slavery?

> As Pharaoh approached, the Israelites looked up, and there were the Egyptians, marching after them. They were terrified and cried out to the LORD. They said to Moses, "Was it because there were no graves in Egypt that you have brought us to the desert to die? What have you done to us by bringing us out of Egypt? Didn't we say to you in Egypt, 'Leave us alone; let us serve the Egyptians'? It would have been better for us to serve the Egyptians than to die in the desert!" (Exodus 14:10–12, NIV)

Wow. This impossible place for the Israelites is one of much anxiety, fear, and hopelessness. They lash out at Moses. But why? What happened to their faith? The Lord had worked miracles through Moses and Aaron, from turning a staff into a snake to turning the Nile blood red. The Lord delivered the Hebrews from all ten plagues. During the Passover, he spared their oldest sons, unlike what happened to the Egyptians. And yet, their faith in the heat of the moment seems nonexistent.

What about Moses?

> Moses answered the people, "Do not be afraid. Stand firm and you will see the deliverance the LORD will bring you today. The Egyptians you see today you will never see again. The LORD will fight for you; you need only to be still." (Exodus 14:13–14, NIV)

Solid leadership. Great faith. Right?

Not so fast.

The Lord's words to Moses are telling, "Why are you crying out to me? Tell the Israelites to move on" (Exodus 14:15, NIV).

Publicly, Moses is a good leader. He is a clear communicator. He does not stutter. He does not need to lean on Aaron to be his voice. But privately, it seems that Moses struggles to believe in God's power to make a way forward. But he brings his fears to the Lord.

Moses knows his dependence on the Lord, even as anxiety fills him in the heat of the moment. There is room for Moses' faith to grow, just as there is for the Hebrew people. But Moses is honest before God, and the Lord guides him through the impossible place and commands him to raise his staff over the Red Sea.

> "Raise your staff and stretch out your hand over the sea to divide the water so that the Israelites can go through the sea on dry ground. I will harden the hearts of the Egyptians so that they will go in after them. And I will gain glory through Pharaoh and all his army, through his chariots and his horsemen." (Exodus 14:16-18, NIV)

What? Lead the Israelites into a vulnerable position? Harden the hearts of the Egyptians—make them really angry? Bring out their pride and self-sufficient confidence? Crazy. Humanly unthinkable. Militarily, suicide. A leadership failure!

Nope. It is just the opposite. This impossible place, this inconceivable plan, is genius. Brilliant and amazing. In this place, the Lord does his most incredible, transforming work in the hearts of his children.

He Tempers Faith

It is in the impossible place where the Lord not only teaches and tests but tempers and strengthens Moses and the Israelites' developing faith.

This dramatic experience forges a more resilient faith to increase their confidence in their good and great God.

This impossible place demonstrates the ultimate power of the Lord and his absolute trustworthiness for all who follow him. The Lord keeps his promises as he rules over Egypt and the Pharaoh—one of the greatest world powers of the time.

The Lord's same power delivers the Hebrews from the shackles of slavery and bondage and protects the Hebrews from deadly plagues. This same power of the Lord holds back the chaotic waters they are about to encounter.

> Then Moses stretched out his hand over the sea, and all that night the LORD drove the sea back with a strong east wind and turned it into dry land. The waters were divided, and the Israelites went through the sea on dry ground, with a wall of water on their right and on their left. (Exodus 14:21, NIV)

Can you imagine? Standing there along the water's edge, feet wet, sand caked over your sandals, and scared to death at when the Egyptians might penetrate the darkness and hem you in. And then you feel the wind and you look over at the Sea, and the waters are forming two distant walls with a narrow path of dry ground to walk through—a miracle of miracles. Something only God could do. "God?! You are there!" you say to yourself as your fear begins to melt and faith and hope and love fill your heart.

Then you are jolted back into reality when your neighbor next to you says to hurry up and get going as the Egyptians are pursuing us.

As the Israelites make their way through the sea on dry ground,

> The Egyptians pursued them, and all Pharaoh's horses and chariots and horsemen followed them into the sea. During the last watch of the night the LORD looked down from the pillar of fire and cloud at the Egyptian army and threw it into confusion. He made the wheels of their chariots come off so that they had difficulty driving. And the Egyptians said, "Let's get away from the Israelites! The LORD is fighting for them against Egypt." (Exodus 14:23-25, NIV)

Pharaoh and his Egyptian army were undoubtedly one of the most powerful military machines of its time. Moses and the Israelites had no chance of survival in their limited human power. But no rival can compare to the Lord—the sovereign creator God of the universe. No cultural advancement, political maneuvering, or military might can overpower his rule and reign.

In obedience, Moses leads God's people into the Red Sea through the dry pathway. As Pharaoh's army pursues, fear drowns their hearts. Confusion and chaos set in as their military apparatus is compromised.

And then the Lord commands Moses, "Extend your hand toward the sea, so that the waters may flow back on the Egyptians, on their chariots, and on their horsemen!" (Exodus 14:26).

The Scriptures tell us that not one of Pharaoh's troops survived—not even one. The whole army perished, just as promised.

This impossible place points to a good and mighty God with whom all things are possible. Moses and the Israelites, with heads spinning and hearts overflowing with joy, must have been so surprised, amazed, and even shocked by what transpired.

That day the LORD saved Israel from the hands of the Egyptians,…
And Israel saw the Egyptians lying dead on the shore. And when
Israel saw the great power the LORD displayed against the Egyptians, the people feared the LORD and put their trust in him and
in Moses his servant. (Exodus 14:30-31, NIV)

This impossible place gave them a glimpse of God's mighty power
and glory, demonstrating his abounding grace and redemptive love for
his people. As thankfulness and celebration filled their hearts, it was just
as Moses said. They only had to be still because the Lord would fight for
them. It was his battle to wage against the Egyptians. It would be their responsibility, with God's gracious help, to replace their natural fears with
a deeply trusting, resilient faith in their good, great, and faithful God.

❦

Mindset Shift in Trials

- Draw a sketch of your own impossible place. Consider emerging areas
  of weakness that have surfaced because of your adversity. Bring these
  areas before the Lord in confession and trust in his provision and
  protection.

- Study Exodus 15's song of deliverance (vv. 1–21), slowly meditating
  on each attribute of God's character. Allow this to lead you into worship, crafting a personal psalm of devotion about an attribute that
  provides you with deep comfort.

CHAPTER 5

HUMBLY LEARN

(Matthew 11:28; Philippians 2:1–11)

Come to me, all you who are weary and burdened, and I will give you rest. Take my yoke on you and learn from me, because I am gentle and humble in heart, and you will find rest for your souls. For my yoke is easy to bear, and my load is not hard to carry.— Matthew 11:28–30

Therefore, if there is any encouragement in Christ, any comfort provided by love, any fellowship in the Spirit, any affection or mercy, complete my joy and be of the same mind, by having the same love, being united in spirit, and having one purpose. Instead of being motivated by selfish ambition or vanity, each of you should, in humility, be moved to treat one another as more important than yourself. Each of you should be concerned not only about your own interests, but about the interests of others as well.— Philippians 2:1–4

PUT ON CHRISTLIKE HUMILITY TO LEARN THE
LESSONS GOD HAS FOR YOU IN THE CRUCIBLE.

❧

One of the greatest enemies of resilience is pride. Humility is its antidote.

It has been said that humility is like a watermelon seed. Just when you think you've got it, it slips from your fingertips.

A spirit of Christlike humility that keeps us anchored, teachable, curious, adaptable, and tenacious is another linchpin to resilience. Yes, we are to always rejoice, love well, stay focused, and deeply trust. Another important practice that sustains personal resilience is to humbly learn.

In this chapter, we discover how to put on Christlike humility to learn the lessons God has for us in the crucible of adversity. There is something the Lord wants to teach us in our journey through hardships as we encounter successes and setbacks, our highest hopes and greatest fears, and in that instance of great victory or hour of defeat.

But first we must understand the nature of humility.

The Nature of Humility

I'll never forget one of our seasoned doctoral students who was full of quiet courage and Christlike meekness. This student, a president of a Latin American seminary in those years, would travel each semester by bus to Guatemala City for a week of in-person training. Every single trip he took from Honduras to Guatemala placed his life in great danger. One semester, he told me over lunch about the Valle de la Muerte, or Death Valley. Death Valley was a particular stretch of road on the way from his home to Guatemala City most notorious for heartless gang-related hijacking, robbing, and even killing of travelers. It was extremely moving that this dear servant would risk his life to come and sit in my class for a week. He was seasoned. He had weathered many storms in life and leadership. He was full of gratitude for the opportunity to learn—he was humble.

This dear servant's countenance radiated a Christlike humility that mirrored the apostle Paul's words to the Philippians. "Do nothing out of selfish ambition or vain conceit, but in humility consider others better than yourselves. Each of you should look not only to your own interests, but also to the interests of others" (Philippians 2:3–4, NIV).

Humility is much more than an important leadership principle for cultivating personal resilience.

Humility is an attribute of God. And this attribute is most powerfully exemplified in the person and work of the Lord Jesus Christ.

And remarkably, as followers of Christ we are called to imitate Christ-like humility in all areas of our life, learning, and leadership.

Paul articulates it so well,

> You should have the same attitude toward one another that Christ Jesus had, who though he existed in the form of God did not regard equality with God as something to be grasped, but emptied himself by taking on the form of a slave, by looking like other men, and by sharing in human nature. He humbled himself, by becoming obedient to the point of death —even death on a cross! (Philippians 2:5–8)

If humility is the antidote to arrogance, then who lives and breathes humility better than our master-teacher, Jesus?

> Come to me, all you who are weary and burdened, and I will give you rest. Take my yoke on you and learn from me, because I am gentle and humble in heart, and you will find rest for your souls. For my yoke is easy to bear, and my load is not hard to carry. (Matthew 11:28–30)

Jesus invites his followers who are weary and burdened to enter his presence to find rest and wisdom in his gentle humble teaching. It was during my time as a Dallas Seminary master's student many years ago, taking Dr. Bailey's Discipleship in the Gospels course, where this passage came to life for me.

Jesus' words render the imagery of two oxen working the land.

One ox is older, stronger, and more experienced. The other ox is younger, with less strength and little experience. If the young ox walks in step with the older one, the load is light. But when it goes its own way, the burden becomes very heavy.

In other words, this is an opportunity for the rookie to become a student, to walk in humility, surrendering his own independent ways to learn from a seasoned, yet gracious and gentle teacher.

In his book *Humble Inquiry*, Edgar Schein reflects on his over forty years of research and writing on organizational culture at MIT. Schein concludes that great leaders cultivate the values of humility and curiosity to move toward asking genuine questions rather than merely telling others what to do.

Schein observes, "All my teaching and consulting has taught me that what builds relationships, what solves a problem, what moves things forward is asking the right questions. In particular, it is the high-ranking leaders who must learn the art of humble inquiry." [7]

As leaders we must ask ourselves, what is driving us? What motivates us to ask the questions we ask? Is it to truly learn in a posture of Christlike humility and others-focused curiosity? Or are we just trying to make a point or push our own agenda?

Part of the heaviness of ministry is that we are still figuring out how to leave our ego at the door. We are still learning how to put on Christlike humility and put off self-protection and pride. It is a pivot away from always having to drive, strive, and control, and toward slowing down, really listening, releasing, and resting in the tension.

Several years ago, I was helping our oldest son, Davey, with a classic "Egg Drop" science project. This project helps students understand basic physics concepts such as gravity, force, and acceleration. The general idea is to have students design a container that will allow an egg to safely drop from varying heights without breaking.

Some students wrapped an egg in bubble wrap; others built many kinds of creative contraptions out of popsicle sticks and other household

---

7 Edgar H. Schein, *Humble Inquiry: The Gentle Art of Asking Instead of Telling*, 2013, 3.

materials. Ours was a little unique. We took an empty cardboard box and carefully stretched about ten rubber bands around the egg at every possible angle. One end of the rubber band was wrapped around the egg and the other end was secured to the box-wall.

We did this from each direction to ensure that the egg was suspended in midair at the very center of the box. Finally, we dropped the egg from about 10–15 feet. When the box hit the ground, the rubber band absorbed the impact and provided some flex for the egg to remain safely suspended—the project was a success. The egg didn't break.

The egg didn't have to do anything but rest in the tension of the rubber bands.

We all too often feel the tension of life and ministry. Sometimes as we are filled with self-reliance, we become stressed because we can't hold it together and the tension is so great we even feel like we might break. But it is through that tension that God stretches our faith until we are forced to rely on him—surrendering all to him. And it is there that we learn to rest in him. We learn true humility. We find rather than us breaking, he is there keeping us from destruction and despair, bringing a resilient peace, joy, and victory.

Pride Can Surprise Us.

I love Ryan Holiday's insight about this subject in his book *Ego is the Enemy*.[8] Holiday highlights three aspects where pride and ego can show itself. The first two aspects he outlines, I get. The third one is a surprise.

He argues first that pride can show itself in our *aspirations*.

When we aspire to something that is rooted in our own self-centered ambition, it can quash resilience. Eugene Peterson describes this tendency in *A Long Obedience in the Same Direction* as "aspiration gone crazy."

You likely have heard the humorous story told of the famous American boxer Muhammad Ali on a flight when the airline attendant asked

---

8 Ryan Holiday, *Ego Is the Enemy*, First Edition (New York, New York: Portfolio, 2016).

him to fasten his seatbelt. He replied, "Superman don't need no seatbelt." She quipped, "Superman don't need no plane."

There is a constant pull to aim for the stars, to prove our ability, to make a difference and change the world. But how much of our leadership aspirations are driven by hubris rather than humility?

There is a common pattern of burnout among leaders. So often, they aspire to something more than God intends. So good things become idols and ends in themselves and at some point, these leaders won't make it. Pride through lofty, unrealistic aspirations becomes their downfall.

Holiday suggests a second way pride can show itself. Again, no surprise. Ego can surface in a leader's *successes*.

Successful leaders all too easily become arrogant, always right, and the fountain of all wisdom. They can be marked by rigidity, no longer able to receive corrective feedback. No longer able to listen. When we become that guru who everyone flocks to for counsel it can become intoxicating. As success feeds and fattens our egos, it suffocates the capacity for resilience.

Okay. Pride surfacing in our aspirations. Yep. Understand that. And ego cropping up in our successes. Got it.

But the third area?

Holiday argues that ego can show up in our *failures*. Fascinating thought.

Here, pride detains leaders from bouncing back. Rather than being flexible, adaptable, and teachable, prideful leaders negatively react to failure. Failure poisons them. Imprisons them. Chains them. These leaders become fragile, inflexible, anxious, and self-protective.

The Value of Trial and Error

I can't help but think back to my childhood, those weeks of learning to ride a bicycle. My first bike was brand new, sparkling bright metallic red with thick treaded white-walled rubber tires. The two black plastic foot pedals carried yellow reflectors on each side. It was quite the challenge when the training wheels were removed. I was learning to ride in a whole new way.

I can still picture it between the barnyard and our home, a large grassy area with a slight slope. My Dad got me started. He believed with time and practice I would be riding before I knew it. He would set me on the bike. My toes could only touch the ground one side at a time. He would hold the back of the seat and send me on my way. There was an exhilarating few seconds and then the unwelcome crash on the forgiving lawn.

Some days I was on my own in learning the art of riding. There were three or four old car tires that we had stacked one on top of the other. This contraption was tall enough that I could use it to mount the bike seat without any help. As I was learning to balance, I fell off that bike countless times. While I couldn't recall what seemed like thousands of wipeouts and crashes and skids, I could count the bruises on my legs. In fact, in some strange way, even amid the frustration of my inability to balance, I took pride in how many bruises I had acquired. At one point I remember counting 30, pulling my pant leg back to show Mom and Dad.

I was determined not to give up. I was dogged if I didn't break in this bicycle and learn to ride it without all the drama. Even in my stubborn resolve there were moments of defeat, not only the bruises that took a toll, but the tears and lots of them, and those moments of throwing the bike on the ground in frustration, and the scrapes, aching joints, and pulled muscles. Sigh.

However, all of this was like my own special school. This school, without me realizing it, was teaching me at a very young age a lesson in humility. A lesson on the importance of trial and error, of not giving up. A lesson in the value of failure as one of life's greatest teachers.

Fast-forward to me learning to lead and preach and shepherd. It was in many ways the same story. I look back at my first church when I was a 20-year-old college student on a four-month summer break serving as an interim pastor in a small rural New Brunswick church—I was just a kid. In fact, during one of the interviews before I took this ministry role, one of the lay leaders said, "You are awfully young. I sure hope we don't have to change your diapers." They were kidding. Sort of. I was trying so hard to be all grown up. I often wore a tie and sports jacket on Sunday morning. One Sunday, I was leading the children's story before preaching the sermon. We gathered all the half a dozen kids at the front of the church. I told a nice Bible story in my pastor voice, trying to demonstrate my maturity. Then one of the sweetest kids shouted, "Scottie, can you tell us another Bible story!" I wanted to shrink.

It was a lot of trials and errors that summer of ministry at Cornhill United Baptist. The previous pastor had been fired. Some on the deacon board were King James only. Gossip in that community spread like wildfire. My eyes were opened to all the brokenness in that small town.

It takes courage, vulnerability, and humility to get up off the ground again and again, whether the attempt to ride the bicycle of life and leadership succeeds, half succeeds for a short ride, or utterly fails. The less it is about me, the better. The more it is about him, the Lord Jesus, the better. Like a hidden treasure buried in the ground, Christlike humility in the face of failure is where resilience is found.

❦

Mindset Shift in Trials

- Take a blank sheet of paper. Make three columns. Outline ten elements of humility from Matthew 11:28–30 and Philippians 2:1–11 in first two columns. In the third column, outline three practices that can help you foster humility and ask the Lord to deepen those in you.

- Write a short paragraph describing a time when you experienced failure and responded with Christlike humility. Describe what happened.

CHAPTER 6

GIVE THANKS

(Psalm 34:7; Philippians 4:4-7)

The angel of the Lord encamps around those who fear
him, and he delivers them. — *Psalm 34:7 (NIV)*

Rejoice in the Lord always. I will say it again: Rejoice! Let your
gentleness be evident to all. The Lord is near. Do not be anxious
about anything, but in everything, by prayer and petition, with
thanksgiving, present your requests to God. And the peace of
God, which transcends all understanding, will guard your hearts
and your minds in Christ Jesus. — *Philippians 4:4–7 (NIV)*

CULTIVATE AN ATTITUDE OF PERPETUAL GRATITUDE

AND THANKFULNESS TO THE LORD.

❧

Joyful thankfulness was as much a part of Paul's resilience as his har-
nessing of affliction, for his own maturing faith as well as bringing
comfort to others. As we stay focused on Jesus in the race set before
us, deeply trusting God to carry us through to the finish and humbly
learning the lessons he has for us along the way, we must also cultivate
a perpetually thankful heart. Otherwise, we could fall far short of the
personal resilience we aspire toward.

A thankful heart in the Lord knows no bounds for a spirit marked by unshakable resilience. This kind of gratitude is what made Paul so extremely effective and impactful.

But how did Paul cultivate such an attitude of unflagging gratitude that is so irresistibly reflected in his letter to the Philippians?

As a prisoner, he was literally straitjacketed by his circumstances at the time of this letter. Several geopolitical storms roiled the Roman Empire. The society and culture of his day was a mess. Even fellow believers seemed to be buckling in their faith. Darkness, anxiety, hatred, evil, hypocrisy were everywhere.

And yet Paul, so full of peace, overflowed with joyful thankfulness. But how?

We find a clue at the end of verse 5: "*The Lord is near.*"

Paul persisted in joyful thankfulness because he knew the Lord's abiding presence. Paul knew that God was with him. Paul knew the perfect character of God in his love and power, and this galvanized his spirit of gratitude.

As we grow in our awareness of his abiding presence, we too can be marked by a persistent and unbroken thankfulness to the Lord.

I'll never forget the cold, wet evening on November 11th back in 1992. I was ministering in Havelock, New Brunswick, Canada, at a small Baptist church. That weekend, the pastor and his family were headed out of town and he asked me to house-sit at the parsonage next to the church.

Driving from Moncton to Havelock was about 45 minutes by car. As I was driving, the rains stopped and the temperature quickly dropped. Before I knew it, the winding backroads in this rural area began freezing over.

Then it happened. There was this one sharp bend where this sheet of black ice—invisible to the eye—coated the road's surface. Deep ditches lined each side. As I drove around the bend, the back end of my old Datsun 210 started to hydroplane right. I attempted to correct the slide but overcompensated, sending the vehicle into a tailspin. Before I knew it the car had stalled on the opposite side of the road facing the wrong direction on the very edge of the ditch.

As the g-forces of the spin shut the engine off, my heart was still racing. But I was so very thankful that I hadn't ended up in the ditch, or worse, collided with another oncoming vehicle.

I reoriented myself, restarted the car, and continued driving toward the parsonage. The remaining way, I drove white-knuckled, at a snail's pace, praying under my breath for God's continued protection. It was a good thing I had slowed down not only because of the patches of black ice, but also, to my chagrin, because a few miles north, a couple of deer crossed the road right in front of me. If I had been driving fast, only God knows what could have happened if I had crashed into a deer.

I finally arrived at the house. Tired and tense. Super grateful for the Lord's protection. To catch my breath, I pressed play on their stereo and turned up the volume, not knowing what music was cued to play.

It was Steve Green's children's song with lyrics taken directly from Psalm 34:7: "The angel of the Lord encamps around those who fear him, and he delivers them."

How timely and descriptive of the Lord's protection. His nearness was so evident. I was so thankful!

Faith over Fear

Paul overflowed with perpetual thankfulness because he knew the Lord was right there with him in his journey of hardship. As we grow in our awareness of his nearness—his abiding presence— we too can live with a spirit of thankfulness to the Lord no matter what.

I love what Paul David Tripp writes in his devotional book *New Morning Mercies*:

> We don't have to live plagued by the anxiety of the unknown. We don't have to go to sleep wondering what the next day will bring or wake up working our way through all the "what-ifs" we can think of. We don't have to seek some means to figure out what we will never be able to figure out. No, we can have rest when we are confused.

We can experience peace in the face of the unknown. We can feel an inner well-being while living in the middle of mystery. Why? Because our peace of heart does not rest on how much we know, how much we have figured out, or how accurately we have been able to predict the future.

No, our rest is in the person who holds our individual futures in his wise and gracious hands. We have peace because we know that he will complete the good things that he in grace has initiated in our lives. He is faithful, so he never leaves the work of his hands. He is gracious, so he gives us what we need, not what we deserve. He is wise, so what he does is always best. He is sovereign, so he rules all the situations and locations where we live. He is powerful, so he can do what he pleases, when he pleases.[9]

When we reflect on God's faithfulness, count our many blessings, and remember how dear and near he is to us, only then can we cease striving in the sea of worry and fear, finding true rest and peace and thankfulness that fosters a resilient, abiding, and obedient faith in our sovereign, good God.

Walking by Faith

This was the case of my sister's resilient faith in the midst of her battle with a rare form of non-Hodgkin's lymphoma. I'm the eldest of five children in our family. My younger sister Angela (we called her Angie growing up) had just given birth to her tenth child (yes, ten!). During that time, the doctors observed swollen lymph nodes which at first were thought to be a result of the pregnancy. However, upon further testing, they discovered an aggressive form of this terrible cancer. After several conventional chemotherapy treatments, the cancer continued to grow.

---

9 Paul David Tripp, *New Morning Mercies: A Daily Gospel Devotional,* 1st edition (Wheaton, Illinois: Crossway, 2014) *February 6th Devotional.*

Then the Lord opened a door for her to receive a novel treatment at the Mayo Clinic.

I'll never forget the time Debbie and I flew to Mayo and visited Angie and her husband Jerome in the hospital and later that day enjoyed a time of fellowship over lunch after her medical appointments. Angie showed hospitality, as she always did, in the hospital. "Did you all need something to drink? We have water, soda, juice. What would you like?" She got up and started walking out of the room down the hall to go to a nearby refrigerator.

"Water is fine." I said. "Are you sure you don't want to rest?" She disappeared for a moment and returned with a couple of bottles of spring water. The doctors came in as Debbie, Jerome, and I sat in her hospital room. They drew some blood and checked a couple of monitors. Then she was freed to go out for lunch.

We went to a Mongolian grill restaurant just a few minutes from the hospital clinic. During lunch, we caught up on our lives, talking about our kids and families. Then with a heart of compassion and being the older brother, I began to ask questions. "Angie, are you taking lots of Vitamin C?" "Is there a way you can hire more help with the kids to lighten your load?" "Are you able to get the rest that you need?" It was a litany of well-intentioned questions and concerns. But then Angie stopped me in my tracks.

She said, "Scott, all these years I have feared that something would happen to me that would keep me from being the mother God wants me to be to my children. And now I am living out these fears. What am I supposed to do? Live in a bubble? I can't. I won't. I'm not going to live by fear. I must walk by faith. For as long as God gives me life I will live by faith." There was silence. She was so right. She had to live by faith. She had to rejoice in the Lord always, knowing that the Lord was with her.

Angie had always shared her faith after coming to Christ at a very young age. Her suffering, her cancer battle, only compelled her to continue to share her faith. She and Jerome shared testimonies of Angie ministering to other folks at Mayo going through their own cancer battles. She was a force. While she never verbalized it, her life shouted *faith over fear.*

She rejoiced in the Lord through the pain and suffering. She knew beyond any shadow of a doubt that the Lord was near, and she found peace there. Angie, like the apostle Paul, kept putting one foot in front of the other with a spirit of confidence in the Lord. Even as the fight against cancer continued, she knew that God was walking next to her, that he was with her and her family. Angie knew the perfect mercy, love, and power of a good God.

Maybe you are battling cancer or a major health setback. Maybe you are struggling with a huge life-changing decision or perhaps you are navigating a family conflict. Whatever it is, we too can be thankful for who God is and how he is sustaining us in the hot coals of the fire on our journey through hardship.

Back in the Garden

I wonder if Adam and Eve's fall in the Garden of Eden is in part their failure to exude thankfulness.

When the Lord created Adam, he made him the caregiver of this beautiful place. He could eat from every fruit-producing tree. God's lavish goodness, provision, and love for Adam is delightfully tangible, extraordinarily evident.

It reminds me of an international student from Ethiopia who visited the US for the first time. My colleague hosted him that first week of his studies and happened to take him to a Walmart Supercenter. This dear brother was in tears as he walked the aisle seeing the rows and rows of fresh produce, fruits and vegetables of every kind and every variety imaginable. He had never experienced such an abundance of food in his whole life.

Adam and Eve were so blessed with such abundance. They could enjoy every kind and variety of fruit in God's Garden with only one exception. They were not to eat from the tree of the knowledge of good and evil. Then Satan entered the situation in the form of a serpent. He took hold of Adam and Eve's outlook and deceptively and intentionally wrought their gratitude into ingratitude, persuading them into questioning the truth of God's Word.

"Did God really say?"

This slippery naysayer planted seeds of doubt about the goodness and nearness of God. It was this demonic spirit of thanklessness that brought sin into the world and inaugurated hardship and suffering, decay and death. The mindset shifted from one of thankful abundance for God's good provision to one of a thankless, self-centered "I deserve more. I deserve better. Why is the Lord withholding this one thing from me?" Soon this evolved into a world of fear, conflict, shame, self-protection, passing blame, covering up, toil, labor, and brokenness. The image of God in humanity is now marred.

In Genesis 3, sin entered the world, wreaking havoc on God's creation and bringing brokenness, suffering, and hardship as a part of everyone's story as Adam's descendants. But how do gratitude and thankfulness contribute to finding resilience?

Once again, the apostle Paul answers this question. Paul understood in the gospel both the transcendence and imminence of God. This filled Paul with thanksgiving, knowing he was the worst of all sinners and yet was forgiven and free from the rule and reign of sin both positionally as well as practically.

Paul deeply articulates in Romans 7 the war that wages between the Spirit and the flesh in his personal struggles. The apostle wrestles with knowing that what he wants to do, he does not do, and the things he does not want to do, he does. His articulated struggle ends with a profound statement:

"What a wretched man I am! Who will rescue me from this body of death? Thanks be to God—through Jesus Christ our Lord!" (Romans 7:24-25, NIV)

Paul knew that God's grace was needed in both his justification as well as his sanctification. God is at work in him through the Spirit to overcome the power of the flesh. With Paul's understanding of his utter sinfulness in contrast to God's abundant goodness in the gospel, he rests in and relishes the free gift of salvation which he did not deserve apart from the grace of God.

Paul's sentiment reminds me of listening to the radio program *The Dave Ramsey Show*. A caller would often compliment Dave's ministry and then ask him how he is doing, and his response would be something like, "I am doing well. Better than I deserve." We don't deserve anything. So in everything we have to learn to perpetually give thanks.

Paul shines brightly as a living, breathing example of spiritual and mental resilience. His testimony reveals how resilience can steel ministry leaders for unusual effectiveness even amid the most relentless hardship in ministry.

❦

Mindset Shift on Trials

- Reflect deeply about a recent hardship you've faced. Take time now to make a list of the top ten reasons for why you can thank God in sustaining you through that difficult season.

- Think about a significant person in your life who brought you security, strength, and protection during adversity. Consider how this might parallel the nearness of God. Outline what happened and what you found to be most comforting.

EMBRACE SCRIPTURE

(Isaiah 40:27–31; Numbers 14:24)

Why do you complain, Jacob?
   Why do you say, Israel,
"My way is hidden from the LORD;
   my cause is disregarded
   by my God"?
Do you not know?
Have you not heard?
The LORD is the everlasting God,
   the Creator of the
   ends of the earth.
He will not grow tired or weary,
   and his understanding
   no one can fathom.

He gives strength to the weary
   and increases the
   power of the weak.
Even youths grow tired and weary,
   and young men stumble
   and fall;
   but those who hope in the
   LORD will renew their strength.
They will soar on wings like eagles;
   they will run and not
   grow weary,
   they will walk and not be faint.
   — *Isaiah 40:27–31 (NIV)*

But because my servant Caleb has a different spirit and follows
me wholeheartedly, I will bring him into the land he went
to, and his descendants will inherit it. — *Numbers 14:24*

TETHER YOURSELF TO THE TRUTH OF GOD'S WORD MORE
THAN THE ANALYSIS OF YOUR PREDICAMENT.

Whether your faith experiences the ultimate test like Abraham; or you wrestle with God like Jacob; or you are at the bottom of the well like Joseph; hemmed in like Moses and the Israelites before the chaotic Red Sea; surrounded by the giants like Joshua, Caleb, and the spies; thrown into the middle of a lion's den like Daniel; cornered into a life and death decision like Esther; trapped in the mystery of heartbreak and suffering like Job; or tormented by Satan himself like Paul—

The reality is you too will endure seasons of suffering beyond belief. And yet the Lord in his grace and goodness promises to walk with his beloved through the crucible no matter how difficult it might seem. And there in that place he breaks us and makes us, he teaches us and tests us, tempers us, and transforms our faith into something beautiful that brings him great glory and grants his beloved children a resilient faith.

Burned Out

This is true for God's people, even those generations that rebelled against the Lord and were led into exile by the Babylonians in 586 BC. This was a time of unrelenting persecution, suffering, torture, death, and slavery for the Israelites. Why? Because they had neglected and forgotten God's Word, and this led them to revolve their lives around false idols. And yet the Lord in his compassion—just like with the apostle Paul—brought his people to their knees in total and utter helplessness and repentance through the grim geopolitical circumstances of a foreign, pagan nation's transitory dominance.

But many of the remnant that pressed on in the fire of God's loving judgment were becoming despairingly weary and worn down. Hopelessness was setting in like a bad infection and for many a red line was moving toward their heart.

"Why do you say, O Jacob, and complain, O Israel, 'My way is hidden from the Lord; my cause is disregarded by my God'?" Isaiah, the prophet of old, echoes the growing sentiment among God's exiled people. In many ways they had not only overlooked God's Word but they had forgotten the true character of the God of Abraham, Isaac, and Jacob only to be consumed by their ever present persecution from the Babylonians and smothered in their harsh circumstances.

There was also a sense that God had forgotten them, left them behind. They wondered why their cries for mercy and forgiveness, and strength, and help had fallen on deaf ears. Their suffering too overpowering, the pain too paralyzing, the shame too harrowing had syphoned all hope.

And in response to this despair the Lord spoke through his prophet Isaiah to address their plight and teach them how they could find renewal.

God's people had to once again tether their hearts and minds to God's Word spoken through his prophets more than focusing on the seeming hopelessness of their predicament. This is something we all have to learn. It can help us stay the course in the darkness of a sinful broken world.

Hope for Tomorrow

Isaiah responds with two rhetorical questions that turn the tables back on the ailing people of God. It is not the Lord who does not know or has not heard—it is his people.

And so the prophet asks, "Do you not know? Have you not heard?"

Human nature lends itself to blaming God for our plight. God knows. God hears. And behind his knowing and hearing is a holy God filled with compassion and a redemptive love for his wayward and broken children.

The Lord—Isaiah reminds his readers—is the everlasting God. Think about that, everlasting. He just is.

His knowledge and power are without end. The Lord is the Creator God over all the earth. There is absolutely nothing outside his purview. He is the grand, eternal architect of the universe. It is impossible for him to grow tired or weary. It doesn't matter what transpires – it cannot exhaust the Lord in his power, goodness, purposes, or pursuit of his children's needs. He knows in such a way that no one can fully fathom his understanding.

Years ago, a dear theology professor, Dr. Burns, exhorted to us students that the beginning and end of knowledge about God leads to worship. That which we understand about God in his person and work can't help but lead us to worship. That which we cannot fathom regarding his character and handiwork also leads us to worship.

The story is told of a group of university students studying for a test in their philosophy course. The students were told that the final exam would consist of one open-ended question and that they would have one hour to answer the question in written form. These students diligently studied. When they sat down to take the exam, they were shocked to read the deep and probing question, "Why?"

In that hour the students frantically wrote their most eloquent answers that integrated all the lectures, readings, and their reflections from that semester. But there was only one student who scored 100% on the examination. And her answer: "Because."

This is a hard answer to receive. Ultimately, no one can fully measure the depth of the mysteries of how and why God works the way he works. But this fact can lead us to trust him in his Word because of what we do know about his wondrous attributes.

In our weariness the Lord is to be our utmost source of strength. In our weakness he is the only one who can increase our power. Are we not foolish to seek out any other source? Even if we are strengthened from the kind words of a friend, or a gift from our spouse, or an act of service from our neighbor, ultimately, we must remember that God in his goodness is the one behind it. Even times when we find a little extra energy from a pour-over cup of freshly brewed coffee, or a pinch of joy in a delicious meal with loved ones. Or the fulfillment found in reaching the next goal in our vocation. All these things may replenish and encourage us in our journey. The Lord, however, is the final source of our vitality, our deep-seated joy, and satisfaction with our lot in life. And we get to know him through the Word in both the Scripture and in knowing the living Word, the Lord Jesus Christ.

It is quite the experience to watch the Olympics. Here we see the fountain of youth, athletes glistening in great feats of speed, strength, dexterity, flexibility, movement, and competition. It is also during these same games that we see many young athletes grow weary during their performances. Their emotions get the best of them under the pressure and they break down in tears after a failed performance. Some have severe accidents, and others, while making every effort toward victory, don't quite make it to the winner's podium.

And so Isaiah contrasts the Lord's untiring, inexhaustible, boundless strengthening power with the most skilled young persons who, while they may be vigorous for a short stint, have significant limitations, lacking in the kind of everlasting power that only the Lord manifests and bestows.

It is only those of us who take every thought captive for obedience to the Lord and wait with expectant hope in him as one who keeps his promises, knows our predicament, sees our pain, loves us, and pursues us to help us rise again from terrible setbacks and losses found in the prison of exile —we are renewed and replace our weakness with strength for new and greater things.

The soaring eagle is a vivid portrayal of renewal in several ways. First, there is this sense of effortless and endless flying at high altitudes safely above all other predatory creatures. Second, some have emphasized the rejuvenation process of the eagles growing new feathers, which gives their wings regenerative longevity. Third, the eagle reminds us of the description in Exodus where the Israelites after 400 years of slavery under Egypt were carried away to freedom on eagles' wings.

The battle belongs to the Lord. Only his power could overcome the Egyptian army in the ancient days of Moses. And now, Isaiah notes that only the Lord can overcome the power of Babylon and remove their suffering, and if they trust in the Lord anew they can fly like eagles, run without becoming weary, and walk without becoming faint because their weakness is exchanged for God's strength as they wait expectantly on his loyal love and for his redemptive measures in his perfect way and timing.

Something Different

The more I reflect on Scripture and the lives of those servants of the Lord who walked with power, the more I realize that they tethered their hearts and minds to God's Word over and above their own predicaments.

These persons knew God's majestic attributes, his trustworthy character, and his loving faithfulness because they riveted themselves to the truth of God's Word.

Caleb, son of Jephunneh, and Joshua, son of Nun, were two such persons. There was something different about them in contrast to the other ten spies as they served Moses and ultimately the Lord on a divine reconnaissance mission.

The reason for their distinction unfolds in Numbers 13.

"The Lord said to Moses, 'Send some men to explore the land of Canaan, which I am giving to the Israelites. From each ancestral tribe send one of its leaders'" (Numbers 13:1–2, NIV).

The Lord speaks. Moses, as God's representative, conveys the Lord's Word to the Israelites. It centers around the Lord's promise to give them the land of Canaan. This idea of the "Promised Land" is not an idea that Moses creates. God made this promise to Abraham, Isaac, and Jacob. The Lord said this land to be explored would be given to the Israelites. It was a promise from a promise-keeping God.

Moses sends out the twelve spies with specific instructions (Numbers 13:1–20). They are to travel through the Negev and into the hill country to assess the fertility of the land and the strength of its inhabitants. The spies are also to bring back some samples of the fruit of the land along with their report.

The spies scout the land for forty days and when they return, they bring with them grapes, pomegranates, and figs—the land is lush and fertile. They confirm that the promised land does indeed "flow with milk and honey!" But then as the spies continue, they urge extreme caution.

> But the people who live there are powerful, and the cities are fortified and very large. We even saw the descendants of Anak there. The Amalekites live in the Negev; the Hittites, Jebusites and Amorites live in the hill country; and the Canaanites live near the sea and along the Jordan (Numbers 13:28–29, NIV).

Then Caleb abruptly interrupts their sour tune and says, "We should go up and take possession of the land, for we can certainly do it" (Numbers 13:30). But the other spies adamantly disagree, "We can't attack those people; they are stronger than we are." And they spread a bad report among the Israelite community about the land. They warn, "The land we explored devours those living in it. All the people we saw there are of great size. We saw the Nephilim there (the descendants of Anak come from the Nephilim). We seemed like grasshoppers in our own eyes, and we looked the same to them" (Numbers 13:31–33, NIV).

It is a rough night of fierce resistance against Moses and Aaron. There is much of drama of weeping and grumbling, and a possible leadership coup is in the making. Clearly this spirit overcome by fear and insecurity ravages the people of God. In their mind there is absolutely no way they can take possession of the promised land (Numbers 14:1–4).

There are Moses and Aaron as they fall face down in despair. And then both Caleb and Joshua muster the courage to speak into the situation even as they tear their clothes in anguish.

> The land we passed through and explored is exceedingly good. If the Lord is pleased with us, he will lead us into that land, a land flowing with milk and honey, and will give it to us. Only do not rebel against the Lord. And do not be afraid of the people of the land, because we will swallow them up. Their protection is gone, but the Lord is with us. Do not be afraid of them (Numbers 14:7–9, NIV).

Caleb was different—very different. Like Joshua, he marched to a completely different drumbeat than that of the other spies and now the entire Israelite community. "But because my servant Caleb has a different spirit and follows me wholeheartedly, I will bring him into the land he went to, and his descendants will inherit it" (Numbers 14:24).

Caleb and Joshua were wholeheartedly tethered to God's Word and covenant, following the Lord by faith. In other words, Caleb was so overcome with the presence, power, and promises of God that any obstacle paled in comparison. This was a stark contrast to the majority of the Israelites who became so overwhelmed by their seemingly insurmountable circumstances that the analysis of their predicament overshadowed God's presence, power, and promises.

Resilience in the Christian life can only be found by those who share this Caleb-spirit to truly know and trust the Lord in his Word to remain pliable, tenacious, and persistent in the mission of God set before us.

Will the personal presence, power, and promises of God overshadow our predicament? Or will our predicament be so magnified that it overshadows our belief in the presence, power, and promises of God?

❦

Mindset Shift on Trials

- Invite a friend who has weathered significant hardship out for coffee or lunch this week. Ask them how they have found renewed strength in Scripture.

- Prepare a short outline for a talk you could give to a small group on the differences between Caleb and Joshua in contrast to the other Israelite spies in their understanding of the goodness and greatness of God in the face of giants.

CHAPTER 8

UNCEASINGLY PRAY

(Acts 12:5)

So Peter was kept in prison, but the church was earnestly praying to God for him. — Acts 12:5 (NIV)

TALK TO GOD AND DEPEND ON HIM FOR POWER
TO BREAK THROUGH EACH TRIAL.

❦

Word spread like wildfire, leaving a dark cloud of fear in its wake as King Herod put James to death with the sword (Acts 12:2). Yes, James—the beloved brother of John, one of the most fearless and faithful leaders of the early church. Herod, indeed, was coming down hard on the growing Christian church. If he could take out the leaders of the pack, perhaps he could snuff out this viral movement and further fuel Jewish support toward his own political ambitions.

Nothing could have been more shocking to the struggling believers than what happened next. Like a fast-moving winter freeze, soldiers seized Peter, arrested him, and threw him into a high security, stone-walled, iron-gated prison with four squads of four soldiers on guard. After the Passover, Herod prepared for a very public trial and timely execution.

As Luke records, "So Peter was kept in prison, but the church was earnestly praying to God for him" (Acts 12:5).

There was no way around it. Peter's life on earth, like James', was about to come to an abrupt, heart-wrenching end. The brothers and sisters of the church knew it. What could they do? Gather together and mastermind a prison break? Or cower and hide, locking themselves in their own homes, scared to death that they could be next? No way. Neither option was their default.

In this place of absolute desperation, they gathered together and turned to the only one who could help them. They turned to the living God of the universe. The creator and sustainer of all things. The master over life and death. The God who delivers. The God who saves. The God of Abraham, Isaac, and Jacob. All that both James and Peter had taught them was not in vain. This ragtag group of Jesus followers learned resilience in the face of great loss and hardship through total and utter dependence on the Lord of all—the Lord over all.

And so as they gathered, they prayed without ceasing, their prayers like the very breath on their lips. Tears soaked their prayers, drowning their fears. Earnest, fervent petitions before the throne of God. Pleading for his grace, mercy, power, and protection over Peter, they beseeched God for his personal, imminent, and supernatural intervention. Like the engineering feat that transforms friction into renewed power or like the father who helped his son move the unmovable log. Like Paul's near-death salvation experience or Moses and the Israelites at the edge of the waters.

Places of desperation lead us to talk to God and compel us to depend on him for power to break through each and every trial.

This was the very place where my former long-time colleague, professor Dr. Stanley Toussaint found himself as he told the story of his wife's life-threatening fall. She had had a full day of activity and had not eaten enough protein. Late that night, she got up to find a snack, but it was too late. Her blood sugar levels dropped dangerously low. She passed out and hit her head. The ambulance came quickly in response to his desperate 911 call. At first, the doctors thought that she had only a mild concussion. However, upon further testing, they discovered an epidural hematoma which required immediate brain surgery. Toussaint writes,

> Her life was hanging in the balance. Normally a person recovers from this kind of surgery in three to five days. After five days my wife was still in a semicoma condition and could not breathe on her own…Fourteen days later her condition was still unchanged. At that time one of the doctors informed me that I better find a nursing home to take care of my wife because I would not be able to care for her.[10]

Understandably, the situation was so distressing for Dr. Toussaint that he couldn't bring himself to go to the regular church prayer meeting that same evening and instead drove himself home where he collapsed on his bed with no words to say.

> For the first time in my life I began to understand Romans 8:26–27, which talks about prayer that can be expressed only in groans. During those two weeks, I had been sending e-mails literally around the world, requesting people to pray for my wife. The next day I went to visit her, and she had suddenly taken a turn for the better. She was able to breathe on her own. From then on her recovery was almost miraculous.[11]

Two weeks later, following further treatments, she was able to go home. And the first thing she wanted to do was cook a meal for her hubby. God in his grace answered Dr. Toussaint's desperate prayer with what the doctor called a miracle. All those who had been praying for Mrs. Toussaint shared in their joy over her healing and restoration.

---

10 Larry Waters et al., *Why, O God?* (Wheaton, Ill: Crossway, 2011), 125.
11 Waters et al., 125.

That is what prayer does. It connects fragile, finite people to the One who holds infinite power.

So Acts 12 describes the budding church—young and old—gathered together for days on end. On its knees, desperately crying out to God to deliver Peter even as they grieve James' sudden and tragic death.

Then the power of God is unleashed. Like a giant tsunami, a force with such intensity nothing can stand in its way. Absolutely nothing.

There is defenseless Simon Peter, entrapped by thick stone walls and unyielding iron gates with sentry units at the main entrance. Locked up, bound with chains next to two intimidating soldiers, there is no way in or out. Peter, sore and exhausted, finally sleeps. In a few short hours, the menacing Herod will prepare for his trial and execution.

There is a threshold where both the duration and intensity of a particular trial pushes us to the brink where in desperation, we talk to God in whole new way.

As the church earnestly prays for Peter, God hears their pleas and answers their prayers.

Suddenly in the thick of the night's darkness a radiant angel of the Lord appears before Peter, striking him on the side, commanding him to get up as the chains fall off his wrists. At first the dumbfounded apostle thinks he is seeing a vision. As they walk through guarded checkpoints, the iron gate at the edge of the city, and finally down length of one street, the angel disappears as Peter comes to his senses. "Now I know for certain that the Lord has sent his angel and rescued me from the hand of Herod and from everything the Jewish people were expecting to happen." (v. 11).

Trials and tribulations can propel us toward a posture of prayer and deeper intimacy with God. It is here that the power of God is often demonstrated in ways that break through strongholds in a supernatural way.

Too Busy and Stressed to Pray

We are a busy and stressed people living in a busy and stressed world. We want to make a difference, find our significance, make a name for ourselves, and if we don't do something, who will? It's a reasonable question. But what if it ultimately is less about what we are doing and more about who we are. What if it is less about me and more about what God is doing through me? What if apart from God's gracious work, we really and truly cannot accomplish anything of eternal value?

Paul Miller so eloquently reminds us in his book *A Praying Life* that prayer's power "comes from being in touch with your weakness. To teach us how to pray, Jesus told stories of weak people who knew they couldn't do life on their own. The persistent widow and the friend at midnight got access not because they are strong but because they are desperate. Learned desperation is at the heart of a praying life." [12]

But how do we learn desperation?

Like the cell phone battery than can no longer hold a charge, all too often we find ourselves tethered to very limited power sources. This short-circuits our prayer life. We don't need to talk to God let alone depend on him as we find our worth, our power, and our strength in a plethora of counterfeits.

How often does our life revolve around the altar of the "My"—my position, my authority, my money, my friends in high places. My influence, my experience, my education. My age, my talent, my tenacity. My attorney, my pastor, my parent, my family. My tech gadgets, my pickup truck, my tools. My physical strength, my health, my personality, my beauty, my charm, my skills, my network, my successes. My, my, my.

But when we hit the walls of reality and depravity in our sin, our brokenness, our dashed hopes, and broken dreams. When our default, illusory sources of power apart from God all fail. When we hit that pain point of feeling like we are drowning in a sea of powerlessness, hydroplaning out of control across the highway of life, hitting the wall with

---

12 Paul E. Miller and David Powlison, *A Praying Life: Connecting with God in a Distracting World*, Revised edition (NavPress, 2017), 98.

no way out. As we grow in an ever-deeper awareness of our personal inadequacy and we acknowledge our dire limitations in the face of life's tangled maze, there is a window of opportunity for building learned desperation leading to fervent prayer.

The resilient leader leverages their desperation to shift their attention from obsession over their weakness to awe over God's strength despite any straightjacketing circumstances. Our thoughts rise above the ominous clouds of hopeless despair. "Wait a second," we remind ourselves, "God is all powerful. Nothing is impossible for him. God is all knowing. Nothing is beyond his comprehension. God is all wise. He gives wisdom generously to those who ask. God is full of love. He is love. He loves me."

Understanding our weakness links us to prayer. Prayer links us to God's power, knowledge, wisdom, and love. It is a moment of experiencing the Lord's comforting presence.[13]

❦

Mindset Shift on Trials

- Think about someone in your community who is known as a prayer warrior. Call them up on the phone and ask them what has most poignantly shaped their commitment to intercessory prayer.

- Journal about a time in the last year when you saw God's power at work in and through prayer.

---

13 Miller and Powlison, *A Praying Life*.

CHAPTER 9

FIND CONTENTMENT

(Psalm 23:1)

The LORD is my shepherd, I shall not be in want. — Psalm 23:1 (NIV)

BE COMPLETELY CONTENT WITH HOW GOD IS
LEADING AND MANAGING YOUR LIFE.

❦

I recall, years ago, watching my late grandfather, Glen, tend to the growing flock of sheep that were closely huddled together in the rugged barn for winter.

There was tenderness in his calloused hands and warmth that radiated nothing less than an abiding love. Each day he would feed them grain and hay. He doctored the sick with penicillin. He woke up often in the early hours to ensure the safe delivery of a newborn lamb. If the pipes froze during a chilling snowstorm, he would be the first to hand-deliver a kettle of water, pouring it along the rubbery, iced pipes that lined the manger.

All of us who worked alongside Grandpa Glen knew of his love for the flock. But it was the sheep that knew it most. The sheep were rarely startled or panicked by his beckoning. They yearned for his voice of loving leadership. They followed his cadence as he led and fed them one day at a time. Who could not trust such a good keeper of the sheep?

Yet on this one icy-cold wintry evening, I was with my grandfather feeding the sheep on our six-generation farm.

One particular ewe forced her way to the grain feeder, and as she greedily gobbled grain, she suddenly jerked backward and began choking. Grandpa motioned for me to go into the stall to help the struggling sheep. I climbed into the feeding area and ran over to the sheep, holding open her mouth, using my two fingers to try to clear her throat.

But I was too late. This poor sheep collapsed and died right before our eyes. I was in shock.

Grandpa Glen just stared at the lifeless sheep, raised his voice, and said, "You foolish sheep!"

Grandpa loved each sheep, he knew their every need, and he had all the resources to tend to their care.

But how did this beloved sheep forget his goodness?

It is an all too convicting question. We can easily forget God's goodness and try to force our needs to be met through expediency rather than through faith and trust in the Lord.

As we lean into verse one of this amazing psalm, Psalm 23, David writes, "The LORD is my shepherd, I shall not be in want." Or, as other translations render it, "I shall not want."

But what does this mean? Words like God's provision, protection, and being content might come to mind. And these are certainly true.

However, I love Phillip Keller's insights in his book *A Shepherd Looks at Psalm 23*. Keller calls us to consider an important question for discovering the whole meaning of *shall not want*—"*Am I completely satisfied with God's [loving leadership and] management of my life?*"

Perhaps you are struggling with finding a sense of contentment and complete satisfaction in a season of unmet expectations. You might be single, longing to find the right one, and all your well-intentioned friends are telling you to become the right one and just trust the Lord. Or maybe you are going through a crazy breakup and might be single again.

It could be that you are newly engaged or just married, and it is taking more than you ever imagined to merge your two very different lives together. Or perhaps you have just celebrated another decade of marriage and yet often feel so misunderstood by your spouse.

Finding satisfaction in your singleness or marriage is tough, and this can also be said of your family. Sometimes discontent surfaces in the stress of raising children, or you try to find your worth and value through your children who let you down. Or the web of relational complexity and conflict of a blended family leaves you despairingly stressed out and discontent.

It could be your job, having to work overtime over and over again, dealing with office politics, being overlooked for a promotion, yearning to work in an area more aligned with your wiring, or being let go in the no man's land of being in between jobs.

Perhaps you are dissatisfied with your financial situation—no matter how much you work, the money is spent before you receive your paycheck. Or it could be that you can't sleep at night because God has blessed you with more money than you know what to do with, and you are trying to figure out how to steward it well (some of you reading this are thinking, "I wish I had that problem").

You might be struggling with hardship in the area of your or a loved one's health setback. It could be cancer, long-haul COVID, or issues of anxiety, depression, or other mental health struggles.

These areas and more are real struggles for us—aren't they? Yet, as we work through Psalm 23, we see three things that can reset discontentment and help us learn to find complete satisfaction in the Lord's loving leadership and management of our life. We can remember three important things that lead us forward on the winding path toward resilience: 1) The Lord loves us fully in his abounding goodness, 2) he knows us completely in his infinite wisdom, and 3) the Lord is able and has all the resources to tend to our every need.

Let's take a closer look at Psalm 23.

Fully Loved

"The LORD is my shepherd, I shall not be in want." (Psalm 23:1). Incredible. The imagery expressed in this timeless Psalm teaches us that God is our good shepherd and we are his beloved sheep. As Roger Ellsworth wrote, "David is asserting that the Sovereign Ruler of the universe has taken up the menial task of shepherding him!" [14]

Sheep are like humans, weak, slow, foolish, and vulnerable. We, like all sheep, need a good shepherd. This Psalmist reminds us that we are Lord's sheep. We can say confidently and intimately that the Lord is my personal shepherd. In other words, I belong to God. I am his. Deeply loved. Fully forgiven. Completely accepted by grace through faith (c.f. Ephesians 2–3). Jesus laid down his life for me on the cross. He saved me from sin. He bought me for a high price. I am his beloved sheep!

I know God personally through faith in him. By faith, we are divinely appointed to receive his love and follow him to the ends of the earth.

In May 2011, we were taking our annual road trip to visit family in Owen Sound, Ontario, Canada. On the first day of our trek, we drove from Dallas, Texas, all the way through Joplin and then spent the night in Springfield, Missouri, off the historic Route 66. The weather that day was full of ominous storm clouds. We slept well and then continued heading north early the next morning.

Later, we would learn the shocking news of a devastating EF-5 tornado that torpedoed its way through Joplin and flattened it. We had been just one day ahead of the destruction.

The day of the storm was a Sunday. One story that was reported concerned a young couple, Bethany and Don Lansaw.

Bethany Lansaw returned home from a dinner theatre play and a quick-frozen yogurt purchase at a local store. She put her yogurt in the refrigerator and found her husband napping on the couch. Suddenly the neighborhood sirens alarmed.

Bethany quickly woke up her husband, Don, and with time running out they collected some pillows and sought shelter in the bathtub.

---

14 Roger Ellsworth, *Opening up Psalms* (Leominster: Day One Publications, 2006), 44.

Bethany covered her face with a pillow, and her loving husband threw himself over her and the bathtub as their house was torn apart. After what seemed like an eternity, the storm passed, and she looked up at her husband, who was turning blue. She desperately sought help, but it was too late.

Don Lansaw had sacrificed his life to save Bethany.

Emily Yoker, in her article in the *Joplin Globe*, articulated it so well: "Don Lansaw will be remembered by his wife, Bethany, as the epitome of goodness."[15]

Don's love for Bethany points us to how God demonstrated his love for us in that while we were still sinners, Christ died for us. Jesus Christ died in our place. This a profound love that God, in his goodness, has incarnated in the gospel.

Completely Known

God not only loves me in his abounding goodness, but my good shepherd also knows me completely in his infinite wisdom.

God knows me. He truly knows me.

He knows my strengths, my limitations, my hopes, my fears, and my past. He knows my present situation and my future. The Lord knows what is best for my soul. And so the Psalmist writes, "He takes me to lush pastures, he leads me to refreshing water. He restores my strength. He leads me down the right paths for the sake of his reputation." (Psalm 23:2-3).

Being created in God's image, we are whole beings who need spiritual, emotional, physical, intellectual, and relational nourishment. We need nourishment from God's Word and empowerment from God's Spirit. We need his guidance as the Lord prescribes faith-deepening, character-building experiences. As the Lord leads us to green pastures, still waters, and right paths, this is where we enjoy a journey that fosters growth

---

15 Emily Yoker, *Joplin Globe*, n.d., joplinglobe.com May 27, 2011; John Stevens, *Daily Mail Online*, n.d., dailymail.com, May 26, 2011.

in character, knowledge, skills, and emotions based on Scripture, God's grace, and empowerment.

The Lord provides guidance and discernment and helps me make wise decisions bringing true rest, nourishment, and refreshment. Every experience on the path God leads us to and through is an opportunity to deepen our faith and build Christlike character. "Lord," we should ask, "what do you want to show me? What do you want to teach me? Where do you want to lead me?"

Abundantly Provided

The Lord, our good shepherd, not only loves us and knows us, but he is a God who has all the resources to attend to our every care. He is more than enough to meet us where we are. He is more than enough to lavish on us more than we ever could ask or imagine.

The Lord is with me in the dark valleys. He sustains me and protects me from my enemies.

I can find peace and contentment in his goodness and mercy every single day of my life and into eternity.

How? Through an "unshakable reliance on His ability to do the right thing, the best thing in any given situation."[16]

The LORD is my shepherd. I shall not want (Psalm 23:1).

♥

---

16 W. Phillip Keller, *A Shepherd Looks at Psalm 23*, Gift edition (Inspirio, 2000), 86.

Mindset Shift on Trials

- One day this week, refuse something you otherwise would enjoy. Contemplate your level of contentment and how you felt without partaking in that particular activity. Then engage in prayer, asking the Lord to strengthen and expand your capacity for contentment.

- Set aside 5-10 minutes to remember all the things you are thankful for despite the difficult things you are encountering. Write them down in bullet form.

CHAPTER 10

FULLY FORGIVE

(Ephesians 4:32; Colossians 3:13)

Be kind to one another, compassionate, forgiving one another,
just as God in Christ also forgave you.— Ephesians 4:32

Bear with each other and forgive whatever grievances you may have against
one another. Forgive as the Lord forgave you. — Colossians 3:13 (NIV)

FORGIVE FREELY, RELEASING YOUR HURT, ANGER, DISAPPOINTMENT,

EXPECTATIONS, AND ANY EXPERIENCE OF INJUSTICE OVER TO GOD.

❦

In this chapter, we explore the importance of learning to forgive fully and freely as another steppingstone toward personal resilience, drawing from the example of the Lord Jesus Christ.

Forgiveness is indispensable to resilience. There is no way around it. Ken Sande underscores that Christians, as the most *forgiven* people, should be the most *forgiving* people in the world.[17]

But how do I overcome an unforgiving heart?

---

17 Ken Sande, *The Peacemaker: A Biblical Guide to Resolving Personal Conflict*, Third edition, revised and updated. (Grand Rapids, MI: Baker Books, 2004), 186.

Researchers have identified the crippling power unforgiveness can have on a person. This toxic emotion revolves around such areas as disappointment with God, with oneself, and with others. Additionally, these unresolved personal hurts are often woven into a broad range of personal experiences.

It has been said that extending forgiveness is like picking a seeding dandelion and with one gentle breath of kindness, blowing the hurt to the wind.

But can forgiveness from the heart really be that simple? Sometimes the hurt, the loss, the disappointment, the betrayal just runs too deep.

A mentor once said, "It is not about getting over it. It is about giving it over."

Resilient leaders relinquish their hurt. They give over their experience of injustice, disappointment, and unmet expectations over to the Lord by understanding God's holiness and their own brokenness and utter dependence on the gracious, redeeming power of God.

One of the greatest examples of this is illustrated in Jesus' story of the Prodigal Son. In this story a compassionate father lavishes his love on his children, including his wayward son who takes his inheritance and squanders it in a life of self-centered, pleasure-focused living. It is only when this son loses everything, left tending filthy pigs in a pigpen, that he comes to his senses and makes the courageous decision to return to his father and beg for his mercy to be treated as a hired hand, unworthy to be accepted as his son.

But for the father, how he must have been deeply heartbroken, hurt, and disappointed in his son –the one he loved and raised and sacrificed for over so many years, who turned away from him. Can you imagine the late nights wondering if his son was okay. The wrestling a father might go through second-guessing the words and actions that may have triggered his son to leave home and the family business. Neighbors asking questions about what happened to their younger son. People making up stories in the community about *that family*.

And yet we know the father's love for his son was deep and rooted. Nothing, absolutely nothing, could diminish his love for his son because that was his nature—kindness, generosity, mercy, and grace, and greatest of these things love. The father's love was not based on anything else. This was his son, and because of who he was and the kind father he was, he chose to love him and to love him unconditionally.

Have you ever been called to love someone that, no matter how you might try and express it whether by word, or deed, or gift, or time, they just can't receive it? It can be exhausting and discouraging. Even for the best of us it can lead to a root of bitterness. But the Prodigal Son story, and the fact that Jesus was its author, both summons and empowers us to a higher calling. A calling that Henri Nouwen calls "wornout" love.

In his book *The Return of the Prodigal Son* Nouwen reflects on the famous Rembrandt painting that vividly captures what the moment would have been like with the wayward son fallen before his father's feet as he asks for mercy, in his shame asking only to be treated as his father's servant.

Here Nouwen reflects, "The true center of Rembrandt's painting is the hands of the father. On them all the light is concentrated; on them the eyes of the bystanders are focused; in them mercy becomes flesh; upon them forgiveness, reconciliation, and healing come together, and through them, not only the tired son, but also the wornout father find their rest." [18]

The Holiness of God

The Scripture declares the holiness of God in contrast to a broken, sin-filled world and people. Our sin is so great that no work or deed, no skill, talent, or ability, no payment can be made to satisfy the just wrath of God. Our own persistent human efforts are worthless and offer no hope of redemption.

---

18 Henri J. M. Nouwen, *The Return of the Prodigal Son*, First Edition (New York: Doubleday & Co., Inc., 1992), 96.

But God broke through and entered our world in the incarnation. Through the person and work of Jesus Christ in his life, death, burial, and resurrection he satisfies the wrath of God and imputes his perfect righteousness on those who place their faith in him. Our standing now is as a sinner saved by grace, positionally made holy. As we reflect on the unpayable debt of our sin and Christ's sacrificial payment on our behalf, we can't help but stand in deep awe, wonder, and renewed hope. Our response can be one of worship, adoration in its greatest form, imitation. So we imitate God's holiness in how we think and live. And we imitate God's love for broken people, including those who may hurt us directly, and we learn to fully and freely forgive others just as we ourselves have been so wonderfully forgiven.

So Paul calls us in Colossians 3:12 to clothe ourselves with "compassion, kindness, humility, gentleness and patience."

Resilient leaders remind themselves that they are not God, but God's chosen. Chosen to be set apart, made holy, on mission as a dearly loved and valued servant of the Most High. This same truth governs their expectations of others. The fellow Christ-follower, is not God, but they are equally God's chosen. If we expect them to be perfect as if they were God, we will drown in hurt and disappointment. Martin Luther of the Reformation was right in his notion that believers are *simul iustus et peccator*, simultaneously holy and sinners.

The Value of Values

A couple of years ago, I had the incredible opportunity to work with a Christian life coach. Over the course of two or three months of interactive Zoom sessions, two inventory assessments, and five Zoom meetings, something transformational happened. I gained deeper self-awareness of my vocational identity, calling, and divine design. But there was something more. It was a particular values-discovery exercise that lit up my world in a new way. Over the years I've been through many of these kinds of learning experiences. But what made this round so intriguing and transformational was taking the values selection a step further. After outlining my top four personal values, I was tasked with articulating several affirmation statements for each of those values. I started the process by brainstorming on yellow sticky notes every value important to me under the sun—faith, hope, love, trust, endurance, Scripture, and so forth. If you've seen my handwriting, it is much like chicken scratch and so each sticky note had this scribbly list of dozens of values. Once they were all exhaustively written down, I began eliminating the ones that overlapped with another or were not as high on my priority list. I know you are wondering what this has to do with forgiveness. Thanks for bearing with me, we will come back to that in just a bit!

Here are my top four personal core values: 1) Love, 2) Trust, 3) Humility, and 4) Resilience. What threads through all these values is the holiness of God and his redemptive love demonstrated in Jesus Christ in the gospel.

Over the holidays this past year, my mind turned to the topic of inner narratives and how they moderate our beliefs and behaviors. These narratives are the stories we tell ourselves; they form an immersive world in the landscape of our minds. I remember talking to a colleague years ago about something of deep concern. He said, "Scott, that's just in your head. Let it go!" Sometimes, we might be conscious of these inner churnings, but other times, we may be clueless. In our world today, there is so much division over things like politics, religion, Mac vs. PC, AI or no AI, you name it—even sincere Christians seem bent on finding something to divide over. What is mindboggling is when believers experience such radical division and conflict. Often, it is an issue of the values they hold and the types of affirmations that underpin them. Over the years, I've witnessed situations where a spirit of unforgiveness permeates, and both sides build fortresses based on their own perspectives. I realize that the narratives we live by shape our capacity to forgive and our ability to give over our hurt, anger, disappointment, expectations, and any experience of injustice to God. This inner narrative of the prodigal son recalling his father's goodness led him to come to his senses and return home. This core conviction also led the father to show unusual compassion upon his son's return—such radical compassion that the older brother struggled to accept his father's actions.

Dealing with Disappointment

Life happens. And it can bring a tsunami of events that bring many kinds of disappointment with God, self, or others, or any combination of the three. As we understand and define our personal core values based on God's Word and woven through the gospel, we become more mindful of identifying and owning our feelings and any false beliefs. These can be confessed and repented of and taken captive to obedience to Christ. We can learn as we receive the Lord's grace and strength to give over any disappointment to the Lord and receive God's supernatural, life-giving forgiveness.

As the book *Hope Grows in Winter* asks, "What do I believe has just occurred? And what is my responsibility to God, myself, and the offending person?" [19]

Mindset Shift on Trials

- Think about a recent conflict where you are holding on to a hurt or disappointment because of an injustice that was no fault of your own. Close your eyes and imagine yourself giving this burden over to the Lord, setting it before him at the foot of the cross. Tell the Lord that with his help, you want to give this over to him.

- Write down a short list of areas that you have found it most difficult to forgive. Now make a list of areas you have experienced forgiveness from others you hurt deeply.

---

19 George Miller and Woodrow Kroll, eds., *Hope Grows in Winter* (Kregel Publications, 2000), 102.

CHAPTER 11

PRACTICE SOUL-CARE

(Exodus 18:17–18)

Moses' father-in-law said to him, "What you are doing is not good! You will surely wear out, both you and these people who are with you, for this is too heavy a burden for you; you are not able to do it by yourself." — Exodus 18:17–18

PRIORITIZE RHYTHMS FOR INTENTIONAL SOUL-CARE THAT
FOSTER SPIRITUAL, EMOTIONAL, AND PHYSICAL WELL-BEING.

❦

A couple of winters ago we had a devastating freeze. It was the kind of a cold spell that paralyzed our city for a few days. Dallas, Texas, generally has mild winters compared to the Great White North where I grew up. Yet this one freeze snapped pipes, toppled trees, and downed power lines, leaving many without electricity. Thankfully our pipes were fine, and we kept safely warm after losing power for only a couple of days. But after that storm, our front yard would never be the same. It turned many shades of brown, becoming like a lifeless dusty desert. Our front lawn, once lush and green, had completely died. It wasn't just dead—it was dead, dead. The heat of summer came and toward the end of the season, we removed the old grass roots down to the clayish soil. Then we ordered a couple of pallets of St. Augustine grass from a local grass company. The whole family joined in the efforts to prepare the soil, lay the grass down like a royal carpet, and then take turns watering it by hand at regular intervals for several weeks. We also decided to plant a beautiful red oak tree. It took some time, research, and effort but the outcome was amazing.

As of this past weekend, we are now through winter and in a season of spring. We spent the weekend once again tending to the new lawn. Trimming, adding some decorative foundation plants, watering the grass and tree. Though we were tired, when we stepped back to admire our handiwork, the results were beautiful. This is a picture of tending and flourishing. It is a portrait of care and cultivation, perhaps it even strikes a chord within the soul for Eden.

I've been burdened for the number of folks we see struggling with significant physical, mental, and spiritual health setbacks. On the surface, they might seem to be making a huge kingdom impact, but they are like Moses trying to do everything on their own and too many are losing ground.

I can't help but hear Moses' father-in-law Jethro's words as he cautions his son-in-law from overwork and under-cultivation, "What you are doing is not good! You will surely wear out, both you and these people who are with you, for this is too heavy a burden for you; you are not able to do it by yourself" (Exodus 18:17–18).

This is one of the most important chapters in finding our way through hardship. We must prioritize rest in our regular rhythms, rest for intentional soul-care that fosters spiritual, emotional, and physical well-being.

It seems that as stress increases in its duration and its intensity, it can quickly siphon the very margin necessary to prioritize the rest we need. It can become a vicious cycle in a downward spiral.

It's like the time I witnessed a single engine Cessna flying over our six-generation farm at an unusually low altitude on a clear day, only to hear the engines sputter and suddenly stall and to watch the plane spiral out of control, crashing in an adjacent field. At that time, there were no cell phones, no internet. In my mind, there was nothing I could do but just watch helplessly with worry for the safety and wellbeing of the pilot and passengers.

Part of the problem begins in our spiritual life. But is it more complex than saying a formulaic prayer, or having a checklist you mark off day-by-day for each devotional you read. It's more nuanced than having an accountability group or prayer partner, though all these are important. The emotional landscape we are immersed in as well as our physical wiring uniquely intersect with our spiritual vitality. So when we think about resilience, we must give considerable thought to embodied soul-care—soul-care that considers the three areas of our whole being, of the spiritual, emotional, and physical. These three areas are like a stack of three overlapping paper towels. While one area may be in more contact with the mess, all of them get dirty. If you are wounded in one, it will bleed over into the others.

While my natural inclination is to argue that it begins and ends with the spiritual life, I'm not sure it is that simple. In these middle years, I've come to a place of conviction that it must begin and end with all three elements in rhythmic unity with habits and disciplines. And most importantly, apart from God's grace, whether common or special, I'm not sure how one can find resilience when hardship pulls at us like unrelenting gravity on a stalling plane.

These next few pages attempt to articulate a matrix or a grid by which you will be able to process your stressors in a way that fuels the disciplines for holistic soul-care and wellbeing.

The first step in this process is to ask ourselves an important question. On a scale of 1 to 10, how intense are my stress levels. The second is to use the same scale to rate the duration or length of time I have been under this intense stress. If we score a 10 on the intensity of the stress but a 1 on its duration, we might think of this as a short, manageable crisis. If we score a 1 on intensity but a 10 on duration, we could consider this a kind of a stressful but minor disruption. However, if we experience a crisis and we score a 10 on intensity and a 10 on duration—in other words a long-term, high-intensity stressor—then this could eventually lead to burnout. This is what was happening to Moses in Exodus 18.

Think of yourself as a bridge. Let's say the bridge was designed to hold a maximum of 100 tons for a duration of 10 hours. And let's imagine there is an accident on both sides of the bridge, stranding trucks and cars for hours and hours. Based on the design of the bridge, as long as the total load of the combined stranded vehicles is under 100 tons, it's okay to withstand the stress load. But if the total weight is over 100 tons, the bridge is going to start to collapse. Also, let's say the total vehicle weight on the bridge is 100 tons, but there is water on each side and it takes rescue crews 12 hours to arrive on the scene. At the tenth hour, the bridge is going to show signs of weakening, leading to eventual collapse.

This is a picture of our life. We need to determine our maximum load capacity for both intensity and duration. The only way we can learn what that is is through a growing sense of self-awareness in the areas of our relationship with the Lord, our emotional capacity, and our physical strengths and limitations.

But here is the challenge. What if life happens in such a way that it is beyond your maximum stress load capacity? And what if that season of stress last for days, or months, or even years?

Richard O'Conner's intriguing book *Undoing Perpetual Stress* brilliantly articulates how we are all too often caged in a state of unhealthy, ongoing stress. O'Conner uses the metaphor of a deer penned in with a leashed predatory canine that, while unable to do any harm, pushes the deer into a heightened state of anxiety simply through its hostile presence. He goes on to explain that if the deer is unable able to free itself from this vicious cycle, it will have a full range of health issues as a result.

This prompts us to an important question we need to ask ourselves: "Am I in a heightened, prolonged state of perpetual stress?"

Whether your first inclination is to respond with a resounding "Yes," or "No," anyone, whether you yourself, a co-worker, a family member or friend, anyone who is in a space of perceived, unending state of heightened anxiety, will eventually shut down their brain's critical thinking center and ramp up what Seth Godin's *Linchpin* calls the "lizard brain." When the lizard brain kicks into gear, critical thinking is inhibited and stress responses of fight, flight, or paralysis take control.

During an army cadet training exercise, we were taking the *Map and Compass* course and were taught methods of self-regulation while experiencing the crisis of being lost. There is an acronym that has stuck with me all these years—S.T.O.P., which stands for, Stop, Think, Observe, Plan.

To strengthen this acronym and our wayfinding skills, we were blindfolded, placed in a deuce, a 2 and ½ ton green-tarped military truck, and transported to an unknown location in the middle of nowhere. We had to find our way back to the main camp using only a map, a compass, and our triangulation skills. The instructors had trained us to normalize the stressful experience of disorientation so that we could think critically and problem solve without inadvertently entering a state of heightened panic, since we didn't know where in the world we were.

A few times now, I've taught my teen and young adult kiddos the S.T.O.P. acronym, applying it not only to being lost but to any crisis. I've also added an extra P for pray. It will be impossible to find your way without prayer, demonstrating complete dependence on the Lord, along with thoughtful, sober minded, spirit-led planning.

In recent weeks, we have suffered an unexpected family crisis with my father-in-law having a debilitating stroke. It is an honor and blessing to serve our extended family as caregivers. However, this setback deepens the level of stress caregiving can bring for the whole family. Over the last several weeks the intensity has increased to a capacity that Debbie and I and our kiddos cannot handle on own. We are working with their senior center to build a team of caregivers to bring a mix of assisted living and skilled nursing to them in their independent living apartment.

This is no small task. As the late Haddon Robinson says, "Aging isn't for sissies." But we are learning about our capacity to care for them in these sunset years as well as our limitations. We are also learning about the challenges of building a team that has the character, compassion, and competency to bless Dad and Mom in their time of need.

We are learning to apply the S.T.O.P.(P). acronym, even though for a couple of weeks the crisis required what felt like 24-hour wrap-around-care—especially by my wife, Debbie.

During this time, and after years of learning my own bandwidth through trial and error, I've had to pull back from the men's discipleship group I was leading and ask another person to preach in my place for a Sunday service. I have also declined two other preaching invitations. Additionally, some of my work hours had to be adjusted. In my younger years, I would have just pushed through and tried to do everything, but after mistakes, I'm more aware of my capacity and have learned to off-load some responsibility so that I can prayerful more wisely manage the crisis at hand.

I've grown to be so thankful for God's goodness and kindness to Dad and Mom. I recognize that ultimately, they are his children. Knowing this helps to ease the weight and anxiety over their wellbeing that I might otherwise try to carry on my own, only to hear Moses' father-in-law, Jethro, saying, "What you are doing is not good. You are going to wear yourself out!"

Why is it that in our culture we promote burning out in an overreaction to rusting out?

Here is the point. Growth in self-awareness is paramount. Not only must we grow in our understanding of the stressors we face in their duration and intensity, but we must also grow in our capacity to manage perceived stress and emotionally self-regulate so as not to inadvertently shut down our critical thinking only to unleash the lizard brain.

❦

Mindset Shift on Trials

- Think about your current stress load. On a scale of 1 to 10, indicate both the intensity and the duration of your stress. Brainstorm ways you can share the weight you carry.

- Take 20 minutes and journal about your current emotional landscape, describing what specific areas need tending and cultivation.

EPILOGUE

Let us not become weary in doing good, for at the proper time we will reap a harvest if we do not give up. — Galatians 6:9 (NIV)

❦

Let's face it—whether today or back in the ancient world of Scripture, life and ministry can get complicated, difficult, and messy.

At the time the apostle Paul wrote his letter to the Galatian church, these believers were experiencing some very real hardship.

The Judaizers were insisting that Christ-followers needed to follow Jewish customs—like circumcision—to be truly saved. This false teaching added works to the gospel in contradiction to what Paul and other pastors had faithfully taught.

As a result of the Judaizers' false teaching, some began to hold back their support of their faithful teachers and leaders. Other young believers became disillusioned by the conflict and gave in to their fleshly impulses in the extremes of legalism or license.

So, Paul urgently addressed this concern head-on, helping these believers find resilience through a mindset shift. The adversity, from Paul's perspective, could first strengthen their support of the gospel-centered teachers, not lessen it. Second, the tension could revitalize their mutual burden-sharing rather than sparking further in-fighting and division. Third, though counterintuitive, the apostle exhorted them to keep on doing good to one another, to keep sowing seeds of the Spirit, to ignore the fleshly lies of the Judaizers, to yield to the Spirit by doing good, especially to those who were a part of the church family.

Paul was burdened that this precious community of faith might become so overwhelmed by the false teachings that they would grow weary and give up. He challenged them to find their way through this hardship, to rise above it and learn from it, and to become stronger because of it, and so he emphatically reminded them to never tire of doing good, to release their situation and results to God, to watch their expectations, and to give their full support to those who serve the true gospel.

This is resilience—that uncanny ability to bounce back from and adapt to difficult challenges. This is the art and science of a mindset shift that transforms the heat and stress and friction life brings into a source of hope, renewal, and transformation.

Therefore, rejoice in your suffering, for God uses it to produce perseverance, character, and hope (Romans 5:3–5). Love others well by being a conduit of the Lord's comfort through your own adversity (2 Corinthians 1:3–4). Fix your eyes on Jesus and his example of running the race with perseverance (Hebrews 12:1–3). Develop a growing confidence in the sovereign care of a good God (Exodus 14:13–14). Put on Christlike humility to learn the lessons he has for you (Matthew 11:28; Philippians 2:1–11). Give thanks always, cultivating perpetual gratitude (Psalm 34:4–7; Philippians 4:4–7). Tether yourself to God's Word over circumstantial analysis (Isaiah 40:27–31; Numbers 14:24). Unceasingly pray and depend on the Lord for overcoming power (Acts 12:5). Forgive fully by releasing your hurt to God (Ephesians 4:32; Colossians 3:13). And prioritize intentional soul-care for spiritual, emotional, and physical wellbeing (Exodus 18:17-18).

Friends, no matter how difficult, daunting, or despairing life gets, it doesn't have to take you down. It is in this place of unimaginable hardship that the Lord breaks us to make us better, humbles us to build up, and burdens us to make us stronger, forming in and through us something more than we could ever imagine.

Have you enjoyed this book?

It's digital version is FREE.
Please, share it in your social media
and use the digital version for your searches

www.ingramcontent.com/pod-product-compliance
Lightning Source LLC
Chambersburg PA
CBHW071903020426
42331CB00010B/2650